SKINNY QUILTS and table runners II
15 designs from celebrated quilters

edited by Eleanor Levie

dedication

To all quilters who go to great lengths for the love of their art and their craft!

acknowledgments

My heartfelt thanks to the hugely talented quilters—all incredibly busy with their own books, classes, and commissions—who generously agreed to squeeze a Skinny Quilt into their packed schedules, and in doing so made this book a work of stunning variety.

Kudos to the consummate professionals at That Patchwork Place, who have transformed my skinny visions into appealing realities:

Mary Green and Karen Soltys, for support and encouragement, and for giving thoughtful and quick responses to my every query, big and small.

Laurie Baker, for going over my instructions with a keen eye and a fine-toothed comb.

Shelly Garrison, for the book design and photo styling, the latter in partnership with Stan Green and Karen Soltys, and set off by Brent Kane's expert photography. How beautifully the chosen pottery, glass, and metal vessels complement the cottons, silks, and wools! I have a feeling many readers will not only rush to create their favorite projects, but also will be letting their Skinny Quilts sweep from walls onto tabletops, and enhancing their soft textures with the hard surfaces of vases, bowls, and basketry.

Skinny Quilts and Table Runners II:
15 Designs from Celebrated Quilters
© 2009 by Eleanor Levie

That Patchwork Place® is an imprint of Martingale & Company®.

Martingale & Company
20205 144th Ave. NE
Woodinville, WA 98072-8478 USA
www.martingale-pub.com

No part of this product may be reproduced in any form, unless otherwise stated, in which case reproduction is limited to the use of the purchaser. The written instructions, photographs, designs, projects, and patterns are intended for the personal, noncommercial use of the retail purchaser and are under federal copyright laws; they are not to be reproduced by any electronic, mechanical, or other means, including informational storage or retrieval systems, for commercial use. Permission is granted to photocopy patterns for the personal use of the retail purchaser. Attention teachers: Martingale & Company encourages you to use this book for teaching, subject to the restrictions stated above.

The information in this book is presented in good faith, but no warranty is given nor results guaranteed. Since Martingale & Company has no control over choice of materials or procedures, the company assumes no responsibility for the use of this information.

Printed in China
14 13 12 11 10 09   8 7 6 5 4 3 2 1

Library of Congress Cataloging-in-Publication Data is available upon request.

ISBN: 978-1-56477-925-0

credits

President & CEO: Tom Wierzbicki
Editor in Chief: Mary V. Green
Managing Editor: Tina Cook
Developmental Editor: Karen Costello Soltys
Technical Editor: Laurie Baker
Copy Editor: Marcy Heffernan
Design Director: Stan Green
Production Manager: Regina Girard
Illustrator: Laurel Strand
Cover & Text Designer: Shelly Garrison
Photographer: Brent Kane

mission statement

Dedicated to providing quality products and service to inspire creativity.

contents

After the runaway success of *Skinny Quilts & Table Runners*, my heart is again racing with excitement over the all-new, totally terrific projects in this book—and I bet yours will, too. Here are 15 more golden opportunities to sample the signature styles of a very diverse group of fresh, world-class quilting talents. As you look over these extraordinary designs, think. . . .

One for the money: These Skinny Quilts will accommodate the skinniest of wallets. They'll help you go green—using what you already have in your stash and saving those greenbacks, or *maybe* splurging on just a few new fat quarters, one-of-a-kind embellishments, or some luscious threads.

Two for the show: Anyone who sees your piece on display—whether it's art on the wall, a tabletop dress up, a dresser scarf, a dramatic touch draped over that high-backed chair, door decor—well, let's just say that friends and family are going to rave on and on about your creativity.

Three to get ready: Yes, get ready to learn something new! Each project is like taking a workshop from one of the quilting world's most popular teachers!

Now GO-GO-GO! You can race through one of these Skinnies in a fraction of the time it takes to make a big quilt. Is your BFF (best friend forever) having a big birthday this weekend? Need extreme decorating in an extremely short amount of time? Within these pages, you'll find the perfect solution, plus great ideas and shortcuts you can apply to all the quilting you do. (Check out the awesome alternatives to binding in "Flowing Lines" on page 48 and "Fabulous Cut Flowers" on page 82.)

While you may have picked up this book because it's got a project by your favorite quilt designer, you'll probably run across the work of someone new to you. Here's your chance to take a test run with something truly *different*. My greatest hope is that you'll find inspiration here and run with it—down the straight and narrow but utterly thrilling path to your *own* Skinny Quilts & Table Runners!

Skinny or not, here we come! Happy quilting,

Elly

Eleanor Levie

outback SUNSET *by Judy Hooworth*

As a quilting celeb in the land Down Under, Judy Hooworth seems to turn traditional quilt blocks on their heads as a natural state of affairs. Here, she cuts triangles from strip sets, producing groups of "tops" and "tails." Tops combine for one block, tails for a second, so, as Judy says, "Simplicity is the order of the day." But she boosts the visual, incorporating bold geometric prints and ingenious Xs in each block. The outcome is hot, hot, hot—like the colors of the canyons and the evening skies at Australia's Red Center.

Finished measurements: 18" x 80"

materials

Fabrics are 100% cotton. Yardages are based on fabrics that measure 42" wide.

⅝ yard of red-and-black striped fabric for border

⅓ yard of turquoise print for blocks and binding

⅓ yard *each* of yellow, red, and black prints for blocks

¼ yard of black-and-white striped fabric for blocks

¼ yard of purple print for blocks

¼ yard of red-and-black dotted print for border

2½ yards of fabric for backing

22" x 84" piece of batting

12" (or larger) square ruler with 45°-angle line

cutting

Cut all strips on the crosswise grain of the fabric (selvage to selvage). Trim selvages.

From *each* of the red and black prints, cut:
4 strips, 2¼" x 42"

From the yellow print, cut:
4 strips, 2⅜" x 42"

From the black-and-white striped fabric, cut:
4 strips, 1½" x 42"; crosscut into 12 identical strips, 1½" x 9"

(Continued on page 8)

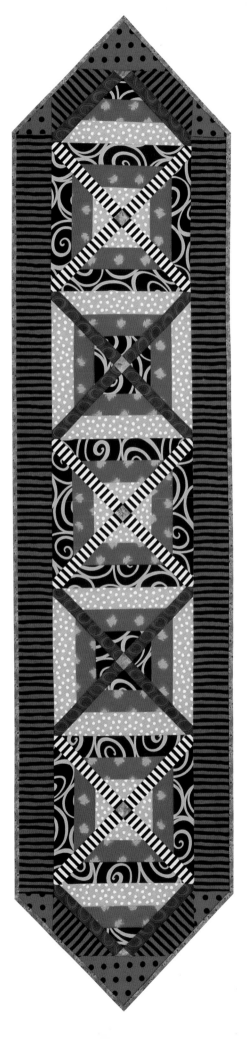

From the turquoise print, cut:

6 strips 1½" x 42"; crosscut 1 strip into 7 squares, 1½" x 1½"

From the purple print, cut:

4 strips, 1½" x 42"; crosscut into:

   8 strips, 1½" x 9"

   4 strips, 1½" x 10"

From the red-and-black striped fabric, cut:

4 strips, 3½" x 42"

1 strip, 2¾" x 42"; crosscut into 4 strips, 2¾" x 9"

From the red-and-black dotted print, cut:

1 square, 6½" x 6½"; cut in half diagonally to yield 2 half-square triangles

1 square, 6" x 6"; cut into quarters diagonally to yield 4 quarter-square triangles

making the blocks

1. Sew a black, a red, and a yellow print strip together along the long edges to make a strip set. Repeat to make a total of four strip sets. Press the seam allowances toward the black strips.

Make 4.

2. Trim the right-hand end of each strip set at a 45° angle, placing the 45°-angle line of the ruler at the top of the strip.

   Note: If you are left-handed, begin by trimming and cutting from the left-hand end of the strip set and work in reverse from the instructions and diagrams.

3. Rotate the strip set on the cutting mat so that the cut edge is on your left and the black strip is on the bottom. Position the "0" corner of the ruler at the top of the strip, aligning the edge of the ruler with the diagonal cut. The 8¼" mark should be lined up with the bottom of the strip. Cut along the right edge of the ruler.

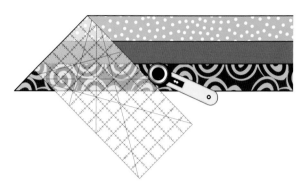

4. Turn the ruler around and cut a second triangle. Repeat the turning and cutting to cut six triangles from the strip. You will have three triangles with the black print on the longest edge of the triangle (A) and three triangles with the yellow print on the longest edge of the triangle (B). Repeat with the remaining strip sets to cut a total of 12 A triangles and 12 B triangles. You will have two left over for another project.

A triangle.
Cut 12.

B triangle.
Cut 12. Discard 2.

5. Lay out four A triangles, four black-and-white striped sashing strips, and one turquoise square as shown. Make sure the same-colored stripe meets the center square. Sew the pieces together, stitching from the tip to the base of the triangles where applicable. The sashing strips will extend beyond the base of the triangles. Press the seam allowances toward the sashing strips. Trim the ends of the sashing strips even with the sides of the block. Repeat to make a total of three A blocks.

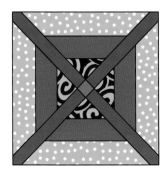

A block.
Make 3.

6. Repeat step 4 to make two B blocks using the B triangles, the purple 1½" x 9" strips, and the turquoise squares.

B block.
Make 2.

Man Your Own Assembly Line!

Focusing on one task at a time will speed up the whole process. Lay out all the blocks, join all the triangle and sashing strips, press the seam allowances, assemble all the blocks, press, and trim all the corners. Before you know it, the work is done!

making the pieced end triangles

1. Sew a purple 1½" x 10" strip to one short side of each of the two remaining B triangles. The ends of the purple strips will extend beyond the base of the triangle. Press the seam allowances toward the purple strips.

2. Sew a turquoise square to one end of each of the remaining purple strips. Sew these strips to the opposite short side of the triangle, matching seams. Press the seam allowances toward the purple strips. Trim the ends of the purple strips even with the base of the B triangles.

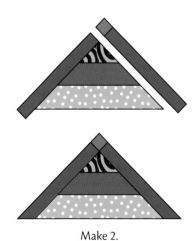

Make 2.

assembling the quilt top

1. Alternately join the A and B blocks into one horizontal row. Center and stitch a pieced end triangle to each end of the row. Trim the sides of the end triangles even with the sides of the joined blocks.

2. For the borders, layer the red-and-black striped 2¾" x 9" strips in pairs, wrong sides together. Cut one end of each pair at a 45° angle. Sew a strip on each side of the end triangles, with the angled end even with the sides of the table runner. Trim across the top of the end triangles, ¼" from the center of the turquoise square.

3. Stitch a red-and-black dotted half-square triangle to the top of each end triangle. Trim the sides even with the table runner angled sides.

Making Your Point Exactly

Before you add each half-square triangle, fold it in half from the base to the point and press lightly to crease. When you pin the base to one end of the quilt, make sure the crease aligns with the point of the joining square directly below it.

4. Stitch two red-and-black striped 3½" x 42" strips together end to end to make one long strip. Repeat with the remaining two strips. Measure the long sides of the quilt top and cut each pieced strip to this measurement. Draw a line 3" from the ends of each strip.

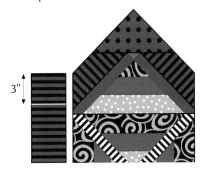

5. With right sides together, align one short edge of each red-and-black dotted quarter-square triangle with the drawn lines on each strip as shown and the other short edge with the long inner edge of the border strip (the triangle is wider than the border strip width at this point; the excess will be trimmed later). Stitch ¼" from the short edge that is aligned with the marked line. Press the triangle up and trim away the striped border fabric ¼" from the stitching line.

triangles at the end of each side border even with the top and side edges.

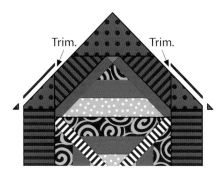

quilting and finishing

Refer to "Quiltmaking Basics and More" on page 89 as needed.

1. Press the quilt top. Layer the backing, batting, and quilt top; baste.

2. Machine quilt in the ditch along all seams. Zigzag stitch along the outer edges of the borders.

3. Trim the batting and backing even with the edges of the quilt top. Use the turquoise print 1½"-wide strips to make and attach a single-fold binding.

6. Stitch these strips to the sides of the quilt top, offsetting the seam line of the red-and-black triangles on the border strips with the outermost seam line of the purple strips by ¼" so that the seams match when sewn together. Press the seam allowances toward the border. Trim the red-and-black

las hojas del OTOÑO (autumn leaves) *by Jane Dávila*

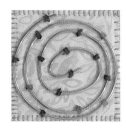

Jane Dávila loves to juxtapose would-be opposites, such as organic curves vs. hard-edged squares, big shapes vs. little ones, deep tones vs. pale backgrounds. "The geometric shapes represent order and structure, while the organic forms are random and loose," she muses. "The combination is far more interesting to me than a composition of just one or the other."

Why not take inspiration from this design and create your own work of art? Just repeat shapes in a rhythm, and balance opposites of color and scale. Consider adding an unexpected element—like these spirals of copper wire from the hardware store, stitched in place with variegated chenille yarn. You'll find that your quilting has suddenly turned into an artful collage!

Finished measurements: 18" x 58"

materials

Fabrics are 100% cotton—mottled prints, hand-dyed fabrics, or batiks. Yardages are based on fabrics that measure 42" wide.

18" x 58" piece of ecru fabric for background

⅛ yard or fat eighth (9" x 11") of pale green fabric for accent squares

8" x 10" pieces of 6 assorted fabrics in rich tones for leaves

⅜ yard of striated tan fabric for binding

22" x 62" piece of fabric for backing

22" x 62" piece of batting

1 yard of 18"-wide lightweight paper-backed fusible web

Threads to match and contrast with fabrics

Fine chenille yarn in variegated colors to match leaves

Fabric markers or pencils for light and dark fabrics

16-gauge copper wire

Wire snips

Rounded needle-nose pliers

Metal file

Tapestry needle

cutting

Cut all strips on the crosswise grain of the fabric (selvage to selvage). Trim selvages.

From the striated tan fabric, cut:
4 strips, 2½" x 42"

appliquéing the skinny quilt top

1. Referring to "Fusible Appliqué the Easy Way" on page 90 and following the manufacturer's instructions, apply the fusible web to the wrong side of the pale green fabric and each of the six assorted leaf fabrics.

2. Trace or photocopy the pattern on page 16 onto paper and cut it out. Place the leaf template on the right side of one of the assorted leaf fabrics. Using a marking tool that contrasts with the fabric, trace around the leaf shape. Remove the paper template and the paper backing from the fabric, and then cut out the shape slightly inside the marked line. Repeat with the remaining leaf fabrics to make a total of six leaves.

3. Remove the paper backing from the pale green fabric. With your rotary cutter, cut 13 squares, 2½" x 2½".

4. Referring to the photo on page 13, lay the leaves on the ecru background piece, evenly spaced and oriented on the diagonal. Place the squares singly, in pairs, or in trios in the empty spaces between the leaves. When you are satisfied with the arrangement, follow the manufacturer's instructions to fuse the leaves and squares in place.

quilting and finishing

Refer to "Quiltmaking Basics and More" on page 89 as needed.

1. Press the quilt top. Layer the backing, batting, and quilt top; baste.

2. Using a light fabric marker or pencil and referring to the leaf pattern on page 16, draw veins freehand on each leaf. Using contrasting-colored thread, free-motion quilt along the marked lines of the veins and the inner edge of the leaves, going over each line twice.

3. Using a blanket stitch or other decorative stitch (if available on your machine) and thread slightly darker than the squares, stitch along the raw edges of each square.

4. Using the patterns on page 17, transfer the leaves, sprigs, and berries to the remaining empty spaces on the background. Free-motion stitch on the lines.

5. Trim the batting and backing even with the edges of the quilt top.

6. Use the striated tan strips to make and attach a double-fold binding.

7. Embellish each pale green square as follows: Cut an 18" to 20" length of wire. Use needle-nose pliers to curl the wire into a flat spiral, with three or four rounds that fit inside a 2½" square. Thread a length of yarn onto the tapestry needle; knot the end of the yarn. Place a wire spiral on an appliquéd square, bring the yarn up from the back, and stitch over the wire at various intervals to secure it in place. End with a small backstitch through the backing fabric only, and bring the needle through this stitch to fasten off. Trim the yarn ends.

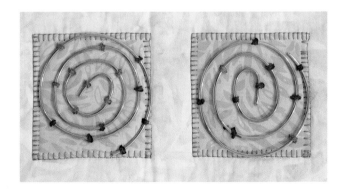

Not the Usual Suspects!

Beautiful buttons, baubles, and beads often find their way onto art quilts. But hey, there's no need to spend big bucks on your embellishments. Found objects from your basement workbench, your desk drawers, or the great outdoors are easy to sew on and guaranteed to add a spark to your creation.

- Plastic-coated cable wire
- Metal washers, as is or painted
- Metal springs
- Small metal hinges or other fixtures
- Common or novelty-shaped paper clips
- Pieces of thin wooden dowel, as is or painted

- Twigs
- Thin pieces of mica
- Seashells, especially those on which clams or sea stars have drilled holes

Bet you can come up with other great ideas!

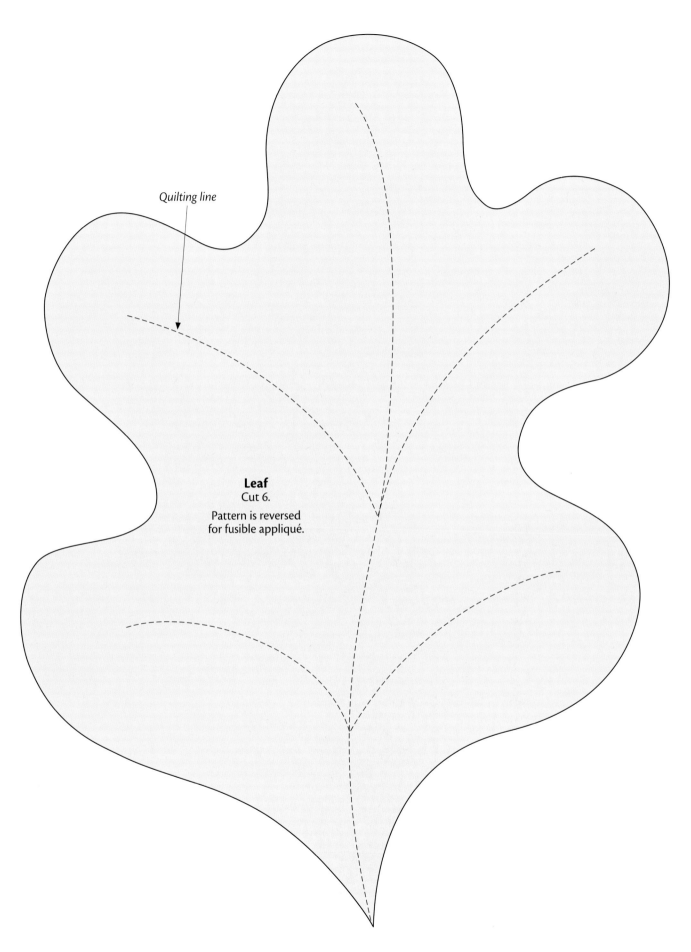

Quilting line

Leaf
Cut 6.

Pattern is reversed
for fusible appliqué.

LAS HOJAS DEL OTOÑO (AUTUMN LEAVES)

Quilting motifs

RUNGS *by Karla Alexander*

As the author of *Stack the Deck*, Karla Alexander was eager to adapt the clever speed-piecing technique she developed for a long, lean piece. Karla shares her steps for cutting blocks and strips and reshuffling the "deck" of fabrics to make surprising and wonderful strip-set blocks. Then, blocks are joined end to end. It's all so stunningly simple that you'll want to continue onward—and upward! As Karla says, encouragingly, "Arrange and modify this ladder design to make your own quilt unique." Scale your ladder to fit your table or space. Customize your colors, too, because any great contrast—like the deep purple batiks and lime green prints shown here—will ensure that you'll rise to success. Why not make this Skinny Quilt for everyone on your gift list? (No one will ever guess you reached the height of creative style so quickly and easily!)

Finished measurements: 16" x 60"

materials

Fabrics are 100% cotton. Yardages are based on fabrics that measure 42" wide.

¼ yard *each* of 3 different lime green prints for blocks

¼ yard *each* of 3 different medium to dark purple batiks for blocks

⅜ yard of fabric for binding

1⅞ yards of fabric for backing

20" x 65" piece of batting

Variegated thread for free-motion quilting

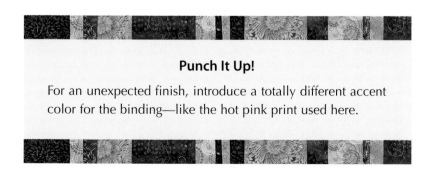

Punch It Up!

For an unexpected finish, introduce a totally different accent color for the binding—like the hot pink print used here.

cutting

Cut all strips on the crosswise grain of the fabric (selvage to selvage). Trim selvages.

From *each* of the 3 lime green prints and the 3 purple batiks, cut:
1 rectangle, 7½" x 17" (6 total)
1 rectangle, 5" x 17" (6 total)

From the fabric for binding, cut:
4 strips, 2½" x 42"

making the blocks

1. Stack the six 7½" x 17" rectangles right side up, alternating purple and green rectangles. Make sure all the edges are perfectly aligned.

2. Turn the stack so the short edges are on the left and right. Measure and cut 3" in from each side edge.

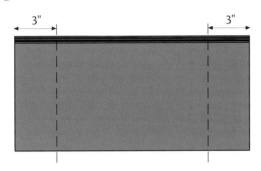

3. Peel off the top layer of the left 3" section and shuffle it to the bottom of the stack.

4. Peel off the top three layers of the right 3" section and shuffle them to the bottom of the stack.

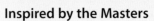

Inspired by the Masters

When considering new color and pattern choices for your "Rungs" design, take a look at the paintings of Mondrian and the architecture of Frank Lloyd Wright.

5. Sew the three pieces of each layer together. Press the seam allowances toward the purple fabrics.

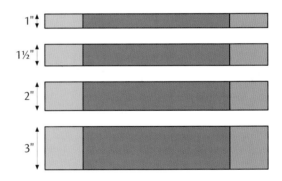

6. Crosscut each layer into one of each of the following width segments: 1", 1½", 2", and 3".

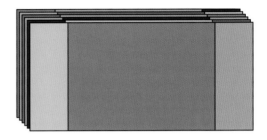

7. Repeat steps 1–5 *only* with the six 5" x 17" rectangles.

assembling the skinny quilt

1. Arrange the segments into six units of five segments each as desired or follow the list below. Alternate purple and green centers in each unit. Pin the segments in each unit together, nesting the seam allowances for corners that meet perfectly.

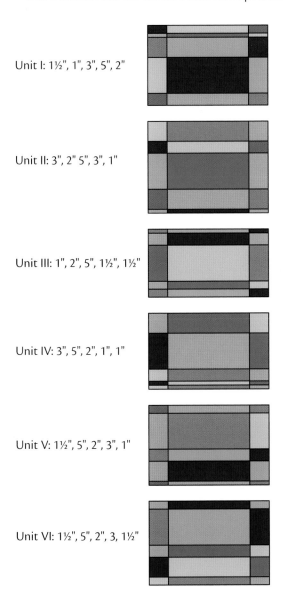

Unit I: 1½", 1", 3", 5", 2"

Unit II: 3", 2" 5", 3", 1"

Unit III: 1", 2", 5", 1½", 1½"

Unit IV: 3", 5", 2", 1", 1"

Unit V: 1½", 5", 2", 3", 1"

Unit VI: 1½", 5", 2", 3, 1½"

2. Sew the segments in each unit together. Alternate the sewing direction as you add each new segment. Press seam allowances toward the darker center sections. Sew the units together.

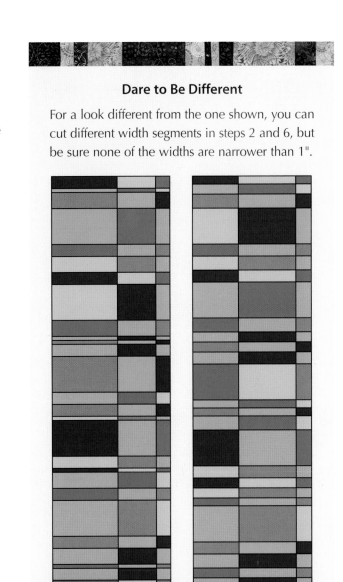

Dare to Be Different

For a look different from the one shown, you can cut different width segments in steps 2 and 6, but be sure none of the widths are narrower than 1".

quilting and finishing

Refer to "Quiltmaking Basics and More" on page 89 as needed.

1. Press the quilt top. Layer the backing, batting, and quilt top; baste.

2. Quilt in the ditch along all seams. Free-motion quilt patterns of spirals, squiggles, or curlicues over each section.

3. Trim the batting and backing even with the edge of the quilt top. Use the 2½"-wide binding strips to make and attach a double-fold binding.

BIRDS of a feather *by Linda Lum DeBono*

"I love bird images," says versatile designer Linda Lum DeBono, "and I drew these expecting to use them in a fabric line." A collection featuring birdie prints is still up in the air but may land on fabric shop shelves sometime in the future. Meanwhile, lime green and chocolate brown in Linda's fresh florals and quiet geometric prints provide the modern color palette here. Quick machine appliqués perch just at either end, guaranteeing that you'll fly through this project. Touches of fashionable texture are unexpected, yet unexpectedly easy, so they'll ruffle your runner, but not your feathers!

Finished measurements: 15" x 53"

materials

Fabrics are 100% cotton. Yardages are based on fabrics that measure 42" wide.

5/8 yard of brown tone-on-tone fabric for ruffles

1/3 yard of light green geometric print for appliqué background

1/3 yard of dark green small-scale floral for plain center

1/3 yard of green-and-brown floral for sashing and ruched center strip

1/4 yard of brown solid for bird appliqués

1 5/8 yards of fabric for backing (less if you want to piece it)

19" x 57" piece of batting

12" x 16" piece of lightweight paper-backed fusible web

12" x 16" piece of stabilizer

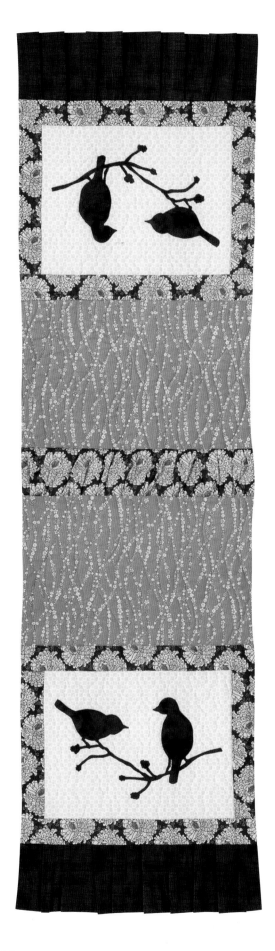

cutting

Cut all strips on the crosswise grain of the fabric (selvage to selvage). Trim selvages.

From the light green geometric print, cut:
2 rectangles, 9½" x 12½"

From the dark green small-scale floral, cut:
2 rectangles, 9½" x 15½"

From the green-and-brown floral, cut:
4 strips, 2" x 9½"
4 strips, 2" x 15½"
1 strip, 3½" x 19½"

From the brown tone-on-tone fabric, cut:
2 rectangles, 8½" x 24½"

making the appliquéd blocks

1. Refer to "Fusible Appliqué the Easy Way" on page 90 and use the pattern on page 25 to prepare two appliqués from the brown solid.

Let Inspiration Take Flight!

Choose another silhouette, customized to your decor. Cut motifs from wallpaper, trace coloring-book illustrations, or put your china face down on a copy machine and blow up the design to fill letter-size paper.

2. Center and fuse one appliqué motif on each light green rectangle, following the manufacturer's instructions. Pin and baste stabilizer behind each appliqué on the wrong side of the rectangle. With a narrow satin zigzag setting, machine stitch around each appliqué. Remove the stabilizer.

3. Sew a green-and-brown floral 2" x 9½" strip to each side of the appliquéd rectangles. Press the seam allowances toward the strips. Sew a green-and-brown floral 2" x 15½" strip to the top and bottom of each rectangle. Press the seam allowances toward the strips.

assembling the quilt top

1. For the ruched center strip, thread 36" of thread onto a needle and knot the ends together. Work a long running stitch by hand along both long sides of the green-and-brown floral 3½" x 19½" strip, beginning and ending ¼" from the ends. Pull the thread to evenly gather the strip to 15½". Machine baste along the gathered sides, ¼" from the edges.

2. Sew a dark green small-scale floral rectangle to each gathered edge of the ruched strip.

3. Sew an appliquéd block to each end of the center, with the birds' heads toward the center.

4. For the ruffles, fold each brown tone-on-tone rectangle in half lengthwise, right sides together. Sew along each short end of the rectangles; turn right side out, pulling out the corners with a pin, and press. Measuring and pinning, make ½" pleats 1½" apart along the raw edges. Baste a scant ¼" from the raw edges to secure the pleats. Pin one pleated ruffle on each end of the runner, with raw edges aligned, and adjust the pleats if necessary. Stitch through all layers, ¼" from the raw edges. Remove any visible basting stitches.

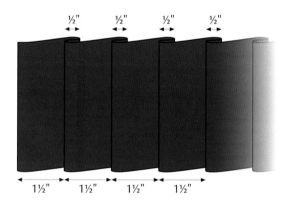

quilting and finishing

1. Place the quilt top on a work surface and fold the ruffles toward the center. Place the backing right side down over the top, and then place the batting on top of the backing.

2. Sew all around the quilt top, making sure not to catch the ruffles in the seam. Leave a 3" opening along one side for turning. Turn the quilt right side out and slip-stitch the opening closed by hand.

3. Quilt as desired. In the quilt shown, Linda used a quilting foot and machine quilted in the ditch along all seam lines and ¼" from the outer edges of the green-and-brown sashing. She followed the curving lines of the small-scale floral in the center area. Finally, she free-motion quilted a meandering pattern along the background of each appliquéd block.

Birds
Cut 2.

Pattern is reversed
for fusible appliqué.

Bright, trumpet-shaped flowers, four-o'clocks got their name because they open in the midafternoon. A motif in an Asian rug was the prime inspiration for this design, although Sue Spargo usually incorporates influences from the wide range of places she has called home. The colors of the African bushveld, the energy of traditional African design, and the lush rolling hills of England all come into play. Sue says, "These early experiences combined to stir my love of primitive arts and crafts."

No doubt the brilliance of her Ohio garden and the fabric dyes she mixes up with her sister also expand her palette. Sue dubs her Skinny Quilt a "table rug"—a pieced wool field for a profusion of hand-appliquéd florals and embellishments. Most of the shapes are cut from slightly felted wool that doesn't unravel, so the edges don't need to be turned under. And there's neither batting nor quilting here! But there *is* a sumptuous warmth that will beckon you to the table for tea at four o'clock, or to your favorite reading corner anytime you like.

Finished measurements: 16" x 72¼"

materials

A felted wool fat eighth measures approximately 12½" x 16". Wool yardage should measure at least 50" wide after felting. Yardages for the cotton, silk, and taffeta fabrics are based on fabrics that measure 42" wide. See "Resources" on page 94 to order a complete fabric pack plus embellishments for making this project, as well as individual pieces or bundles of dyed wool.

½ yard of felted yellowish green wool for background

1 fat eighth *each* of 4 assorted felted green plaid wools for pieced border

1 fat eighth *each* of felted slate plaid, blue, teal, and black wool for appliqués

⅜ yard of green raw silk for background

1 fat eighth of navy dotted cotton fabric for appliqués

1 fat eighth of fuchsia polka-dot cotton fabric for appliqués

4½" x 5½" piece *each* of felted wool in royal blue, bluish green, bluish green striped, gray, gray striped, aqua, purple, mustard, fuchsia, orange, and orange plaid for appliqués

4½" x 5½" piece of periwinkle blue taffeta for appliqués

4½" x 5½" piece of burnt sienna velvet for appliqués

Scrap of fuchsia tweed felted wool for appliqués

19" x 76" piece of heavy wool coating for backing (can be pieced from different wool pieces)

Threads: red and black topstitching; cotton in colors to match cotton appliqués and rickrack; size 12 wool/ acrylic blend in colors to match wool appliqués

2½ yards of blue jumbo rickrack

Heishi beads: 12 black, ⁵⁄₁₆" diameter; 11 red, ¾" diameter*

#11 straw needle

#24 chenille needle

Appliqué pins

*These have one hole; sew-through buttons may be substituted.

cutting

From the yellowish green wool, cut:
1 rectangle, 10¾" x 21¾"
1 rectangle, 10¾" x 15¾"
1 rectangle, 10¾" x 10¾"

From the green raw silk, cut:
1 rectangle, 10¾" x 13¾"
1 rectangle, 10¾" x 7¾"

From the 4 assorted felted green plaid wools, cut:
3¾"-wide strips, totaling 200" in combined length

assembling the quilt top background

Most wool and silk fabrics do not have clearly right and wrong sides, so use whichever side you prefer. To sew, pin pieces together, and then stitch ⅜" from the raw edges. Press seam allowances open using steam and a pressing cloth.

1. Stitch the yellowish green wool and green raw silk pieces together as shown to make the quilt top center.

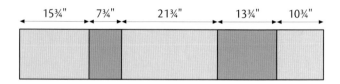

2. Make a border using the green plaid 3¾"-wide strips: Cut one strip to 10¾" long and stitch it to one end of the joined center. Piece together a random combination of the remaining strips to equal the measurement of one long edge; sew the pieced strip to the side of the center. Continue around the center in this manner, joining strips and sewing them to the remaining two sides to form the quilt top background.

making and positioning the appliqué shapes

1. Refer to "Getting the Folk-Art Look" at right to cut one 5½"-diameter circle (A) from slate plaid wool, one 2½"-diameter circle from orange wool (C), and one 2"-diameter circle from fuchsia tweed wool (D).

2. Trace the patterns on pages 30 and 31 onto freezer paper, using a light box or sunny window if necessary. For pieces that overlap each other, extend the edges to the short dashed lines. Freezer-paper templates are reusable, so begin by making one template of each piece and make another when needed, if necessary, for cutting multiple pieces.

3. Lightly press the freezer-paper templates onto the fabrics indicated on the patterns. For velvet and cotton fabrics, press the template onto the wrong side of the fabric and cut out the shapes, adding ¼" seam allowances all around; for all other appliqués, cut out along the edges of the freezer-paper template. Remove the freezer paper from each piece.

4. Referring to the photo on page 27, position pieces A–I in place in alphabetical order, pinning to temporarily secure each piece.

5. Position the rickrack stems. Lay a length of rickrack from the largest flower at one end to the largest flower at the other end, placing it under pieces as necessary. Add shorter rickrack lengths to make stems for the remaining large flowers.

6. For the remaining stems, cut ¼"-wide bias strips from the teal wool. Position these stems at an angle from the main rickrack stem, placing the ends under the rickrack and trimming them to the lengths desired. Place additional shorter stems at an angle from these stems.

7. Position the fuchsia J triangles at the ends of the teal stems closest to the large flowers at the ends of the background. Arrange the K and L pieces singly or in pairs at the ends of several of the remaining teal stems.

8. From the black wool, cut 54 squares, 1⅛" x 1⅛"; round the corners to form circles for the berries. Position these on the remaining teal stems, reserving some berries to fill in open areas later.

Getting the Folk-Art Look

For berries, don't rely on perfectly round, freezer-paper templates. Instead, do like Sue and cut the circles freehand, starting from strips and squares. Some shapes will turn out more oval, some more oblong. Such variations just add to the folk-art charm.

9. Scatter leaves M–P along the stems.

10. Position three royal blue J triangles above each large flower.

11. Adjust the various elements to achieve balance and a variety of slanted lines. Add the remaining berries, filling in wherever there is an empty spot. Make sure stem ends are tucked under flower heads or other stems.

stitching the appliqués

1. To appliqué wool shapes, use the chenille needle and wool thread in a color to match appliqués and whipstitch along the raw edges. Needle-turn appliqué the remaining shapes using matching cotton thread and the straw needle.

2. Blindstitch the rickrack in place by hand.

assembling and embellishing the skinny quilt

1. If you're piecing the backing, make it the same size as the quilt top. Place the top and backing right sides together.

2. Stitch all around the quilt ⅜" from the edges, leaving a 6" opening along one long side. Clip the corners and turn the quilt right side out. Slip-stitch the opening closed.

3. Steam press the quilt from the backing side.

4. Referring to the photo, sew three black heishi beads to each fuchsia J triangle and one red heishi bead *each* to 11 orange L triangles. Use a single strand of matching topstitching thread, knot the end, and make a backstitch behind where each bead will be. Bring the needle up through the center hole and then down at the edge of the disk; repeat three more times to form an X.

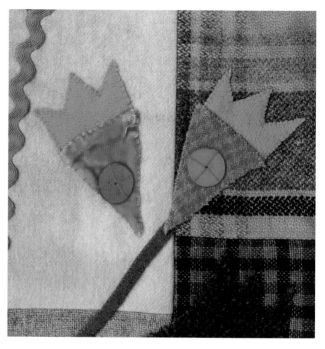

Leaves
Cut a total of 4 from navy dotted cotton
and 15 from assorted bluish green and gray wools.

M

O

N

P

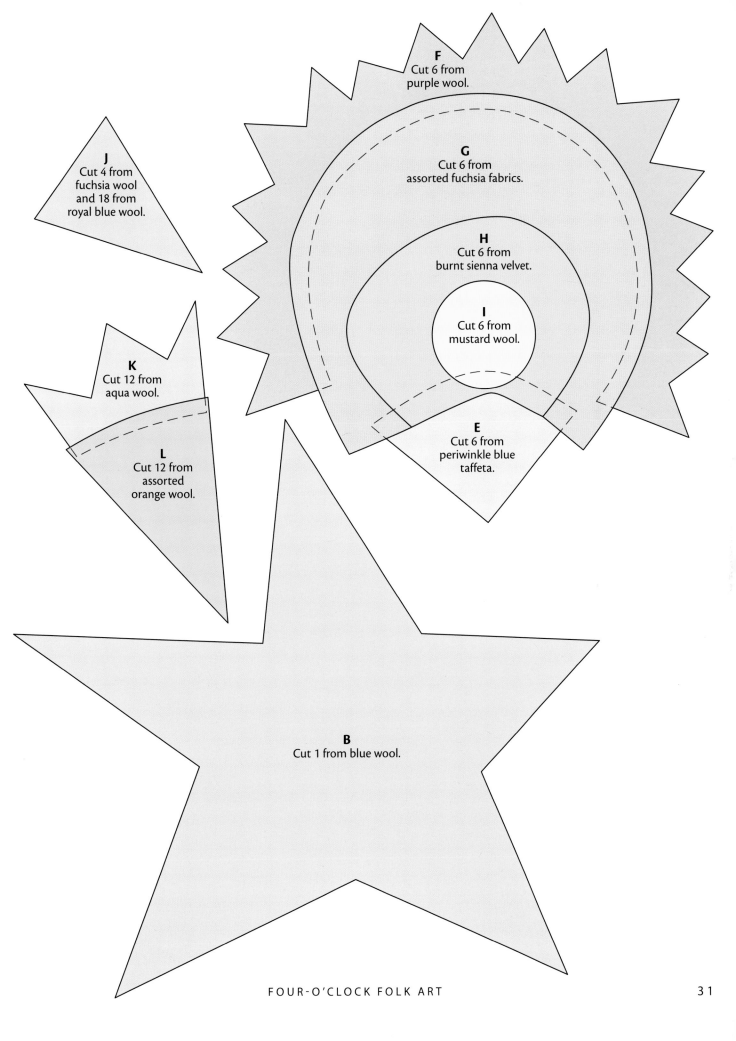

F
Cut 6 from
purple wool.

G
Cut 6 from
assorted fuchsia fabrics.

H
Cut 6 from
burnt sienna velvet.

I
Cut 6 from
mustard wool.

E
Cut 6 from
periwinkle blue
taffeta.

J
Cut 4 from
fuchsia wool
and 18 from
royal blue wool.

K
Cut 12 from
aqua wool.

L
Cut 12 from
assorted
orange wool.

B
Cut 1 from blue wool.

FOUR-O'CLOCK FOLK ART   31

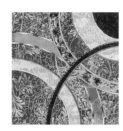

Good heavens, the techniques that make this Skinny shine are pure genius—yet they couldn't be easier. It's simply a matter of cutting arcs and playing around with them. Lonni divulges that the design was "inspired by my love of 'outer space' movies," but the result also reminds her of a lunar path chart. Fabrics, all from the Lonni Rossi collections (see "Resources" on page 94), feature subtle visual textures—mottled, striated, crackled, swirly, and sophisticated shades of purple, green, brown, and gray. Adding to the cosmos are twinkles of light reflected by metallics in some of the fabrics and threads. In any season you'll be over the moon with pride when spreading out this quilt under your roof.

Finished measurements: 17" x 77"

materials

Fabrics are 100% cotton. Yardages are based on fabrics that measure 42" wide. See "Resources" on page 94 for ordering fabrics or a fabric pack, plus the Cut A Round tool.

3⅛ yards of dark purple fabric for arcs, borders, backing, and binding

½ yard *each* of 7 assorted subtle prints in purples, browns, and yellowish greens, some with metallic gold accents, for arcs and backgrounds

2⅝ yards of 17"-wide lightweight paper-backed fusible web

21" x 81" piece of batting

Rayon and metallic threads in colors to complement fabrics

Cut A Round tool for cutting 6"- to 19"-diameter circles OR a yardstick compass set OR string, pencil, and pushpin*

Silk pins

Appliqué foot

See "Circling Around" on page 92.

cutting

Cut all strips on the crosswise grain of the fabric (selvage to selvage) unless instructed otherwise. Trim selvages.

From the dark purple fabric, cut:
5 strips, 2" x 42"

From the *lengthwise grain* of the remaining dark purple fabric, cut:
1 piece, 21" x 81"
2 strips, 3½" x 78"
2 strips, 6" x 19"

From *each of 6* of the 7 assorted subtle prints, cut:
2 squares, 11½" x 11½" (12 total)

From both the remaining subtle print and the remaining dark purple fabric, cut:
1 square, 11½" x 11½" (2 total)

From the fusible web, cut:
8 squares, 11¼" x 11¼"

cutting the arcs

1. Referring to the manufacturer's instructions, carefully center and then press a fusible web square to the wrong side of one square from each of the subtle prints, and the dark purple 11½" square (8 total). You should have ⅛" of unfused fabric all around the square.

2. On the paper backing of each of these squares, mark a point in one corner, ⅛" from the paper edges on two adjacent sides. Because the fusible webbing is slightly smaller and centered, this point should be ¼" from two adjacent sides of the fabric square.

3. If you are using the Cut A Round tool, place a fused fabric square paper side up on a cutting mat, with the tool on top. Align the center hole of the tool with the marked point on the square, and the ends of the curved slots along the sides of the square. Rotary cut along the 6" slot to create a quarter circle with a 3" radius. Then, rotary cut along every other slot (8", 10", 12", 14", 16", and 18") to make 2"-wide arcs. Repeat for the remaining fused squares, altering the radius and width of the arcs you cut to create variously sized quarter circles and arcs as narrow as ½" and as wide as 3½".

If you are not using the Cut A Round tool, use one of the methods described in "Circling Around" on page 92 to mark smooth quarter circles and arcs. Always begin at the marked point rather than the corner. Scribe quarter circles with 3", 4", 5", 6", 7", 8", and 9" radii. Repeat for the remaining fused squares, altering the radius and width of the arcs you cut to create variously sized quarter circles and arcs as narrow as ½" and as wide as 3½". Cut out each piece along the marked lines using fabric scissors.

Use one or more of the methods described above to mark 10½"-radii arcs on the paper backing of each square. Cut out all the pieces along the marked lines using fabric scissors. Keep all the pieces sorted by fabric.

arranging the blocks

1. Arrange the remaining six 11½" squares that have not been cut apart into one row on a design wall or other flat work surface.

2. Choose a few arcs from the other fabrics in several different sizes and place them on the first background square to form a concentric quarter-circle pattern. Maybe let the background square show through between some of the arcs. Pin the arcs in place, inserting silk pins straight down into the layers.

3. Next, arrange quarter circles, arcs, and leftover pieces on the remaining background squares. Referring to the photograph on page 33, try various compositions, placing arcs so they radiate out from two opposite or adjacent corners of a block or from three corners. Allow some arcs to overlap others. To create a sense of flow, allow the curves of some

arcs to continue from one block to another. Add the largest and thinnest arcs last, using them to outline and emphasize the curves of some fabric arcs or bisect others, adding complexity to the design. Continue playing with the blocks until you like the arrangement.

Free-Form Frolic

Lonni says: "At least in the beginning, don't fret about placement; just have fun with the shapes and the colors and textures!"

4. At this point, take a picture (or six cell-phone camera shots!) of the blocks. If you forget where pieces belong as you're securing them, you can refer to your photo(s). Working with the arranged blocks one at a time, peel away the backing paper from each piece and recompose the design on your ironing surface. Then fuse the pieces in place with a hot, dry iron. Replace each block on the design surface.

assembling the skinny quilt

1. Check the fused blocks to be sure they are still square and true, and trim all of them to the same size if necessary.

2. Sew the blocks together as arranged. Press seam allowances toward the side with the fewest layers to avoid bulk.

3. Center and sew a 3½" x 78" border strip to each long edge. Press the seam allowances toward the border, and trim the ends even with the row of blocks. In the same way, add a 6" x 19" border strip to each end.

quilting and finishing

Refer to "Quiltmaking Basics and More" on page 89 as needed.

1. Press the quilt top. Layer the backing, batting, and quilt top; baste.

2. As an extra precaution to keep the layers from shifting, use a walking foot to stitch in the ditch around the border and in the seams between blocks.

3. Using an appliqué foot, secure the edges of every fused circle section with stitching. Work a line of straight stitching first, close to each raw edge. Then go over each raw edge with satin stitching using a variety of rayon and metallic threads and zigzag widths. With each new thread, take time to check your tension on a quilt sandwich scrap before stitching on your project.

4. Using an appliqué or patchwork foot, add echo quilting in some unquilted areas, staying parallel to curves or straight lines of the blocks.

5. Using a darning foot and a variety of threads, free-motion quilt meandering stitches on the borders and a few of the wider arcs or background areas.

6. Using an appliqué foot, satin stitch around the outside edges of the blocks, once with a wide stitch, directly on the seam, and a second time with a very narrow stitch, using the presser foot to stay a consistent ¼" beyond the wide satin stitching.

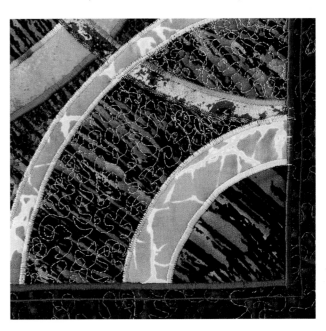

7. Trim the quilt batting and backing even with the edge of the quilt top. Use the dark purple 2"-wide strips to make and attach a single-fold binding.

the DAHLIA is a DIVA   *by Julie Popa of Sunflower Hill Designs*

Cropped by the frame of the on-point blocks, giant blossoms appear even larger than they actually are, unrestrained and bursting with style. Texture also adds drama. With a talent for hip, fresh home decor and quilt design, Julie Popa pops her head into a stash that's eclectic in fiber types and far-ranging in color. "When I'm deciding what type of fabric to use, I let color be my guide," she confides. "If I have the perfect soft peach in wool, or a great olive green in pinwale corduroy, that's what I use."

Julie never disdains classic quilter's cotton, though, especially for backgrounds, setting triangles, borders, and backing. Don't have just the right color in any fabric? Then just put some pieces on a "dye-it," as Julie did to get a nice, deep brown for the framing pieces. Camouflage that ugly or bland old cloth and put it to use in a supporting role. With a Skinny Quilt this easy, quick, and showy, it's a sure bet you'll have an overnight star on your hands—or on your table.

Finished measurements: 14¾" x 66"

materials

Yardages are based on fabrics that measure 42" wide. For appliqués, ¼-yard amounts can be fat quarters (18" x 22") and ⅛-yard amounts can be fat eighths (9" x 11"). Fabrics for appliqués can be 100% cotton, wool, wool blend, or synthetics. All other fabrics are 100% cotton.

⅝ yard of brown print for setting triangles and end borders

½ yard of ecru print for background

¼ yard *each* of aqua, light orange, medium orange, reddish orange, red, and dark brown solids for appliqués

¼ yard of teal print for setting triangles and one large flower (C) appliqué

⅛ yard *each* of dark red, dark brown, medium green, and olive green fabrics for appliqués

Scraps of khaki fabric for appliqués

½ yard of brown solid for binding

1 yard of fabric for backing

19" x 70" piece of batting

1 yard of 17"-wide fusible web

THE DAHLIA IS A DIVA

cutting

Cut all strips on the crosswise grain of the fabric (selvage to selvage). Trim selvages.

From the ecru print, cut:
3 squares, 13¼" x 13¼"

From the teal print, cut:
1 square, 7⅜" x 7⅜"; cut into quarters diagonally to yield 4 quarter-square triangles

From the brown print, cut:
2 strips, 1½" x 42"; crosscut the strips into:
   4 rectangles, 1½" x 6"
   4 rectangles, 1½" x 7"
2 strips, 3½" x 42"; crosscut into 4 rectangles, 3½" x 16"
2 strips, 4¾" x 42"; crosscut into:
   2 rectangles, 4¾" x 11"
   2 rectangles, 4¾" x 15"

From the brown solid, cut:
5 strips, 2½" x 42"

making the blocks

1. Place one of the ecru squares on a cutting mat, turned on point. Using a clear ruler with a 45°-angle line, measure in 2" from one corner; rotary cut along the ruler's edge. Repeat on the opposite side. Repeat with the remaining two ecru squares for the block backgrounds.

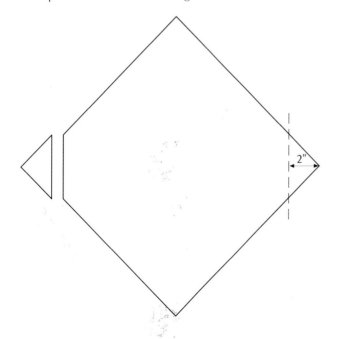

2. Refer to "Fusible Appliqué the Easy Way" on page 90 and use the patterns on pages 41–43 to make three of each appliqué shape. You will use one of each shape in each block, so vary the fabrics for each of the three shapes needed, referring to the photo on page 37 as necessary. Use a pressing cloth and a longer fusing time to apply the web to thicker fabrics, such as wool or corduroy.

3. Arrange the three ecru background pieces in a row, with the points meeting. Referring to the photo and the assembly diagram on page 40, position appliqués on each piece. Work in alphabetical order but insert the edges of pieces C, I, J, and K under the large B flower pieces, and insert the ends of G and H under F. Insert the ends of L and M under the K pieces. Allow flowers to extend past the edges of the background piece. When you are satisfied with the arrangement, fuse the shapes in place. Be sure to protect the ironing surface from the fusible adhesive of appliqué pieces that extend beyond the block! After fusing, trim the extending ends of the flowers even with the sides of the block.

Trim appliqués even with sides of background.

4. Using gray or brown thread and a machine blanket stitch, zigzag, or other decorative stitch, sew around the edges of each appliqué.

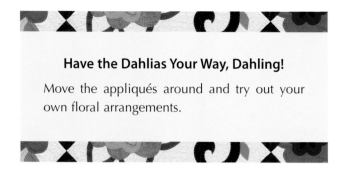

Have the Dahlias Your Way, Dahling!

Move the appliqués around and try out your own floral arrangements.

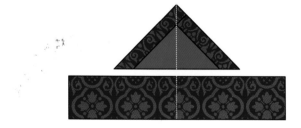

making the setting triangles

1. Pin and stitch a brown print 1½" x 6" rectangle to one short edge of a teal print quarter-square triangle. Unless otherwise indicated, always press seam allowances toward the brown fabric, or toward the most recent piece added. Pin and stitch a brown print 1½" x 7" rectangle to the adjacent edge of the triangle. Press as before. Trim the ends of the brown rectangles even with the base of the triangle. Repeat to make a total of four triangle units.

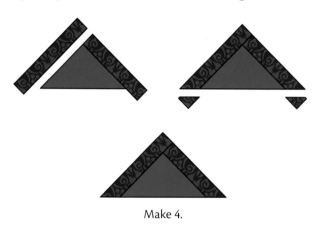

Make 4.

2. Fold each triangle unit in half along the base; crease the fold. Also fold the four brown print 3½" x 16" rectangles in half crosswise and crease the fold.

3. Matching the creases, pin and then sew a rectangle to the base of each triangle unit. Press, and then trim the ends of the brown rectangles even with the sides of the triangle units to complete the setting triangles.

assembling the skinny quilt top

1. Arrange the three blocks in a row, point to point. Rotate the blocks to produce the best balance and rhythm. Pin and sew a brown print 4¾" x 11" rectangle to one edge of each end block; press the seam allowances toward the rectangles. Add a brown print 4¾" x 15" rectangle to the adjacent side of each end block. Using a rotary cutter and ruler, trim the ends of the brown print rectangles even with the short sides of the blocks.

2. Position the setting triangles next to the blocks to create three diagonal rows. Pin, and then stitch the blocks and setting triangles together in each row. Press the seam allowances toward the setting triangles. Stitch the rows together. Press the seam allowances in one direction.

quilting and finishing

Refer to "Quiltmaking Basics and More" on page 89 as needed.

1. Cut the backing fabric in half lengthwise, remove the selvages, and sew the two pieces together end to end; press. Press the quilt top. Layer the backing, batting, and quilt top; baste.

2. Using thread to match the fabrics, free-motion quilt as desired, or as follows. Echo quilt around the flower and leaf appliqués. Quilt a wavy line along each scroll shape (piece K). Trace and follow a continuous-line pattern on each teal setting triangle. Work a fill pattern of small curlicues over the background areas of the block, including the openings of each large flower outer petal (piece C). Work a linear pattern of large curlicues along the wide, brown rectangles.

3. Trim the batting and backing even with the edges of the quilt top. Use the solid brown 2½"-wide strips to make and attach a double-fold binding.

Patterns are reversed
for fusible appliqué.

C

B

A

41

F

E

D

Patterns are reversed
for fusible appliqué.

H

G

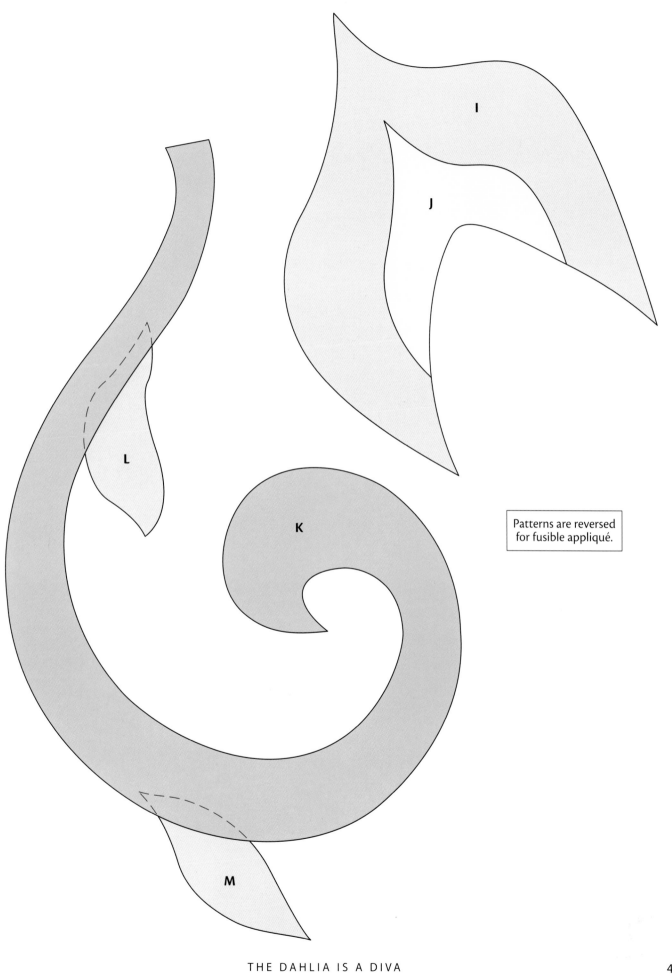

I

J

Patterns are reversed
for fusible appliqué.

L

K

M

starry NIGHT *by Karen Costello Soltys*

Karen Soltys predicts clear skies ahead for anyone making this table topper. Although piecing diamonds and setting in triangles can be challenging, Karen navigates the way to piece one of her favorite blocks on point. Appropriately for this designer, who has been transplanted from one coast to another, East meets West as scraps of hand-dyed fabrics combine with an Asian indigo. Karen muses, "While the stars are reminiscent of Amish patchwork, they take on a whole new light against the Japanese print of the setting triangles." Why not put together fabrics that reflect your regional background and unique personality? Spread out over your table, your Skinny Quilt will warmly invite guests into your world.

Finished measurements: 15" x 69"

materials

Yardages are based on fabrics that measure 42" wide.

½ yard of indigo print for setting triangles and end borders

Scraps of 10 assorted blue, red, brown, and olive solids (approximately 9" x 22" *total* of each color) for blocks

½ yard of red solid or hand-dyed fabric for binding

1 yard of fabric for backing

19" x 73" piece of batting

cutting

Cut all strips on the crosswise grain of the fabric (selvage to selvage). Trim selvages.

For the blocks

Select three of the assorted fabrics for each of the five blocks—two for the star points and one for the background. You can use the same fabric more than once in different positions if desired.

From *each* of the solids for the star points, cut:
1 strip, 2½" x 20" (10 total)

From *each* of the solids for the 5 block backgrounds, cut:
4 squares, 3½" x 3½" (20 total)

1 square, 5¼" x 5¼" (5 total); cut into quarters diagonally to yield 4 triangles (20 total)

For the remaining pieces

From the indigo print, cut:

2 squares, 16" x 16"; cut into quarters diagonally to yield 8 triangles

4 strips, 1½" x 14"

From the red solid or hand-dyed fabric, cut:

5 strips, 2" x 42"

piecing the blocks

1. From each of the assorted solid 2½" x 20" strips, cut four 45° diamonds, 2½" wide.

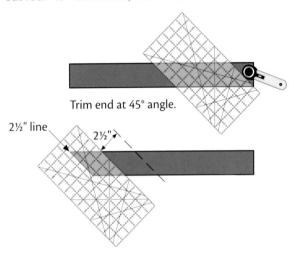

Trim end at 45° angle.

2½" line   2½"

2. Using the four diamonds from each of two different-colored fabrics, sew one diamond of each color together to make four pairs, starting and stopping stitching ¼" from the points.

Start and stop stitching ¼"   Make 4 pairs
from each end of seam.   for each block.

3. Sew one edge of a 3½" background square to one diamond point, starting ¼" from the inner point and sewing to the end. Remove the units from your machine and align the adjacent side of the square with the next diamond point. Again, start stitching ¼" from the inner point and sew to the end. Repeat with the remaining pairs.

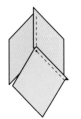

Set in square.

4. Sew the pairs of star points together to make two half blocks, starting ¼" from the inner point and sewing to the end.

Make 2.

5. Sew a background triangle between the joined star points. Start ¼" from the inner point (the black dot on the illustration) and sew to the ends.

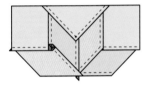

Set in triangle.

6. Sew the two half stars together, matching the inner points, and then sew the remaining two background triangles between the star points to complete the block.

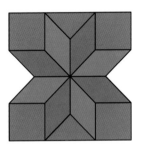

Join star halves.

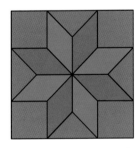

Set in 2 remaining triangles
to complete block.

7. Repeat steps 2–6 to make a total of five Eight-Pointed Star blocks. Press well, and then square up the blocks to measure 10".

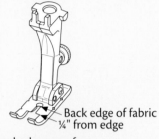

Simple Setup for Set-In Seams

Here's a tip to make set-in seams easy to manage. Just start and stop sewing ¼" from the points to leave the seam allowances free for stitching to the next piece in the block. You can either use a small ruler or a template to measure the distance, and then mark the starting and stopping points with a pencil. Or, perhaps you have a patchwork presser foot with ¼" markings that will make the work a cinch.

Back edge of fabric ¼" from edge

Notched presser foot

assembling the skinny quilt top

1. Arrange the blocks on point on your design wall or the floor in the order you'd like. Lay the indigo setting triangles between them.

2. Sew the blocks and triangles together in diagonal rows. Start sewing by aligning the square corner of the triangles with the corners of the blocks. The triangles are cut oversized to let the stars float in the background, which means the triangle points will extend well beyond the ends of the blocks.

3. Sew the rows together, matching seam intersections.

4. Using the indigo 1½"-wide strips, align one end of a strip to the block at one end of the table runner. Stitch the strip to the block and the setting triangle extension. Press, and then trim the end of the strip at a 45° angle to align with the setting triangle. Repeat for both sides of both ends.

Trim.   Trim.

quilting and finishing

Refer to "Quiltmaking Basics and More" on page 89 as needed.

1. Cut the backing fabric in half lengthwise, remove the selvages, and sew the two pieces together end to end; press. Press the quilt top. Layer the backing, batting, and quilt top; baste.

2. Quilt as desired. Karen used two strands of ecru embroidery floss and a large Sharp needle to hand quilt the star blocks to give the feel of traditional sashiko quilting. The setting triangles are quilted by machine in a repeating clamshell pattern.

3. Trim the backing and batting even with the edges of the quilt top. Use the red or hand-dyed 2"-wide strips to make and attach a double-fold binding.

flowing LINES *by Elizabeth Rosenberg*

From the trail of a drop of rain as it travels down a window to nature's slender pod casings to soft dunes of golden sand, Elizabeth Rosenberg has always been fascinated by graceful, organic lines. With this Skinny Quilt, she expresses her passion for curves in silk dupioni, adding a luminous elegance to what might alternately be captured in quilter's cottons. No matter what type of lightweight fabric you use, Elizabeth is reassuring about the easy methodology: "There's no need for patterns, no need for pins, no need to clip or mark curves, and definitely no need to feel afraid!" To the contrary, this immersion in improvisational piecing will have you going with the flow!

Finished measurements: 13" x 55" (can vary according to preference)

materials

Unless otherwise indicated, fabrics are 100% silk dupioni (see "Resources" on page 94). Yardages are based on fabrics that measure 42" wide. Fat quarters measure 18" x 21".

2 yards of yellowish gold (R#44) for quilt top

1 fat quarter *each* of Poppey (copper), Burgundy, and Brige (ivory) fabric, or 3 contrasting fabrics of your choice for quilt top

2⅛ yards of fabric for backing and facing

17" x 70" piece of batting

Gold, burgundy, beige, and off-white thread for quilting

½"-wide heavy-duty paper-backed fusible-web tape

cutting

From the yellowish gold fabric, cut:
4 strips, 6" x 70½"

From *each* of the 3 fat quarters of contrasting fabrics, cut:
4 rectangles, 5½" x 18" (12 total)

From the fabric for backing and facing, cut:
2 pieces, 17" x 70"

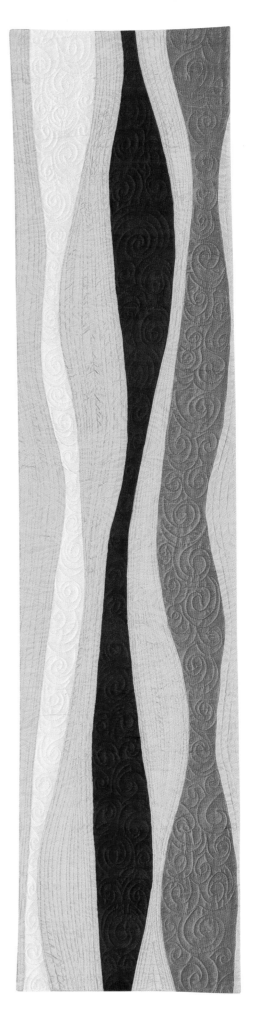

piecing the quilt top

1. Sew the four rectangles of one contrasting fabric together end to end along the short edges to make a piece that measures 5½" x 70½". Repeat with the remaining two contrasting fabrics.

2. Place a strip of yellowish gold fabric vertically over a large cutting mat, also positioned vertically. Place a piece of ivory or your choice of contrasting fabric alongside and to the right of the yellowish gold strip, overlapping the background fabric by approximately 3½". Make sure the fabrics are completely smoothed out.

3. Using a rotary cutter but no ruler, make a gently curving cut through both layers where they overlap, but not beyond it. This curve should have shallow hills and valleys, not steep ones. As you rotary cut, keep your non-cutting hand well away from the open blade of the rotary cutter. Begin your cut on the cutting board, not on the fabric. Before you shift the cutting mat to keep it underneath the cutting action, check to be sure you've cut completely through both of the fabrics. As you finish, extend your cut beyond the end of the fabrics and onto the cutting board. Do not move either fabric after making the cut.

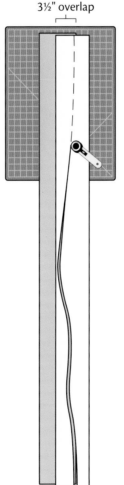

3½" overlap

Rehearse the Curve

Nervous about going directly into freehand cutting? Try this first: Tape together freezer paper to measure 3½" x 70½". Draw several curves along the dull side of this strip using a different colored pencil each time. Stay loose and free with your drawing. Choose the curve you like best, and go over it with permanent marker. Use a hot iron to press the strip shiny side down over the overlapped fabric, and follow the winning curve with your rotary cutter.

4. Lift up the excess ivory fabric to the left of the cut, and throw it into your scrap bin for another project. Without repositioning the ivory fabric, slip out the excess yellowish gold fabric from underneath the ivory fabric to the right of the cut.

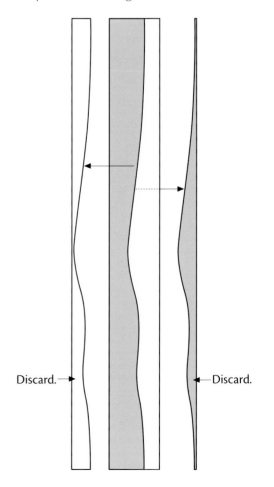

Discard. →   ← Discard.

5. Carefully flip the ivory strip over atop the yellowish gold fabric. Some areas will be "valleys" on the top fabric, and some will be "hills." Begin sewing at the top of the strips using a ¼" seam allowance. To sew along a valley, pull the top fabric slightly so it meets the edge of the yellowish gold strip. Focus your attention only on the ¼" to ½" section where you're actually sewing. For hills, keep the seam flowing smoothly: Shift the ivory piece to the left, in order to keep the raw edge of the ivory strip even with the raw edge of the yellowish gold strip. Working on a small area at a time, stitch the hill of the top piece to the valley of the bottom piece. It will be helpful to use one hand to maneuver the top ivory strip and the other hand to guide the yellowish gold strip on the bottom.

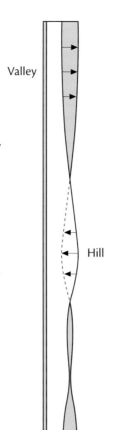

Valley

Hill

Hakuna Matata—No Worries

Don't even give a passing thought to the rest of the strip—all those gentle hills and valleys will wait patiently until you get to them. As Elizabeth often tells her workshop participants, "We'll cross that bridge when we come to it!" When you finish stitching, if one strip ends up a little longer than the other, just trim the ends even.

6. Finger-press first, and then use the tip of the iron to press the seam allowances toward the darker fabric.

7. Place the piece on the cutting mat with the yellowish gold fabric to the left. Using a long acrylic ruler, trim the left edge straight and true.

8. Place another yellowish gold strip on top of the ivory strip, overlapping it by approximately 3½". Continue as described in steps 3–7, alternating contrasting-colored strips and background strips. When you're done, cut the right long edge so it's parallel with the left edge and trim the top and bottom of the quilt top so they are even and true and the quilt is the length desired.

quilting and finishing

Refer to "Quiltmaking Basics and More" on page 89 as needed.

1. Press the quilt top. Layer the backing, batting, and quilt top; baste.

2. Quilt as desired or as follows. Working on the yellowish gold areas, use matching thread to echo quilt (machine stitch flowing lines along the length of the quilt). On the contrasting fabrics, use matching thread to free-motion quilt spirals or curlicues that meander along the flowing shapes.

3. Trim the batting and backing even with the edges of the quilt top.

4. With right sides together, center the 17" x 70" facing rectangle over the quilt top. Baste it in place with long stitches or pin baste. Flip the piece over, and stitch ¼" from the backing edges. Trim the raw edges even with the quilt. Clip across the corners. Then, carefully cut into the facing fabric, leaving only a 3"-wide frame all around (appliqué scissors are helpful for this step). Turn the frame edges to the back of the quilt. Clip ¼" into the corners, and then turn the raw edges ¼" to the wrong side; press. Insert strips of fusible-web tape under the pressed edge, and follow the manufacturer's instructions to fuse the facing in place. Alternatively, slip-stitch the pressed edge to the backing.

blushing ASPENS *by Frieda Anderson*

Every day, Frieda Anderson walks her dog, George, in the 22-acre woods near her home. So it should come as no surprise that over the last several years, trees and leaves have appeared more and more frequently in Frieda's quilts. "Like a leaf pulled to the ground by the forces of gravity, I am drawn to their subtle curves and seasonal colors," she muses. Here she shares a simple leaf block, straight pieced except for two expressive curves. Master that process and repeat it for a whole pile of leaves in various shapes and sizes. Fall in with Frieda's example using her own hand-dyed fabrics (see "Resources" on page 94), charted map for the design, and "Frie"-motion quilting; or pick your own fabrics, seasonal colors, mosaic arrangement, and quilting patterns. Any way you work it, you'll make Mother Nature blush with pride!

Finished measurements: 18" x 54"

materials

Fabrics are 100% cotton. Yardages are based on fabrics that measure 42" wide.

2 yards of variegated grayish brown fabric for background and border

1 yard of variegated reddish orange fabric for leaves

¼ yard of variegated bluish green fabric for stems

³/₈ yard of goldish brown batik for binding

1⅞ yards of fabric for backing

22" x 58" piece of batting

Freezer paper

Spray starch

Washable glue stick

Fine-point permanent marker

cutting

Cut all strips on the crosswise grain of the fabric (selvage to selvage). Trim selvages.

From the goldish brown batik, cut:
4 strips, 2½" x 42"

leaf samples

Before you jump into the pile of leaves in the project, walk through the technique with a couple of sample blocks. Full-size patterns for a Large Leaf block and a Small Leaf block are given on page 57. Rake up some scrap fabrics and let's go!

1. Trace the Large Leaf pattern onto freezer paper. Use a marker plus a ruler for all straight lines and mark on the shiny (waxy) side. By marking on the shiny side, you will create a motif with the same orientation as the pattern.

2. Working on a cutting mat and using a ruler, rotary cut along the outer lines of the freezer-paper template. Rotary cut the pieces apart on the traced lines and label as shown. A rotary cutter with an 18 mm blade makes it easier to cut the curved lines.

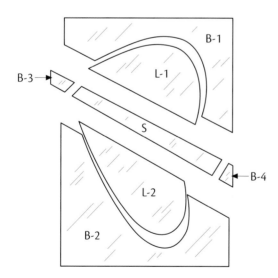

3. Place all the B pieces shiny side down on the wrong side of the fabric you've selected for the background, leaving ½" between pieces and ¼" around the outside edges. Press lightly with a hot, dry iron to adhere the pattern to the fabric.

4. Using a rotary cutter, cut out each piece ¼" beyond the freezer-paper edges; use a ruler for all straight edges. With sharp scissors, clip the leaf's curve around each of the two background pieces at approximately ¼" intervals, clipping up to but not into the freezer paper. Fold back these clipped tabs along the curve of the freezer paper and finger-press. Then spray the edges with starch and press with an iron.

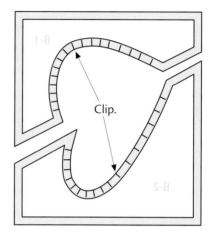

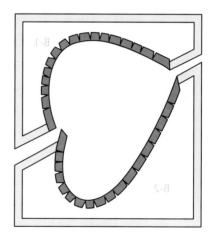

5. Place the freezer-paper leaf shape L-1 shiny side down on the wrong side of the fabric you've selected for the leaf, with straight edges along the grain. Press lightly. Cut out around the shape, leaving at least a generous ½" margin all around.

6. Run a glue stick along the seam allowance that you spray starched on the curved edge of the B-1 piece. Working from the template side, place L-1 over B-1, matching up the openings, and then press with a hot, dry iron. The glue stick will adhere the fabrics together around the leaf.

Let cool, and then remove all the freezer-paper pieces.

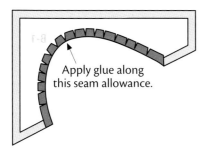

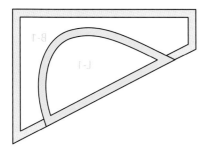

7. Flip up the background fabric under the curve of the leaf, and sew along the leaf curve using the crease as your sewing line. Go slowly and encourage the fabric to curve smoothly. Repeat to join the B-2 and L-2 pieces. Then trim the leaf fabric to align with the background fabric edges, leaving ¼" seam allowances.

8. Place the S freezer-paper piece shiny side down on the wrong side of the fabric you've selected for the stem. Press lightly. Rotary cut ¼" beyond the freezer paper on all sides.

9. On the edges of pieces B-3 and B-4 that will be adjacent to the stem piece (S), fold the seam allowances to the wrong side and apply the glue stick. Adhere the stem piece to these pieces, aligning the freezer-paper pieces. Press and let the glue dry. Then lift up the seam allowances, remove the freezer-paper templates, and stitch along the creases to join the pieces.

10. Position the three pieced units alongside each other. Place one side of the stem section against one side of the leaf and background unit, with right sides facing and raw edges even. Sew, leaving ¼" seam allowances; press the seam allowances toward the stem. Trim these seam allowances to ⅛". Repeat on the other side of the stem to finish the block.

11. Follow the same procedure with the Small Leaf block, eliminating the stem.

making the blocks

1. To re-create the design shown here, enlarge the pattern on page 56 to 500%. This will give you full-size patterns for each of the various leaf sizes. Alternatively, now that you know the process for creating the leaves, try your hand at drafting your own leaf shapes.

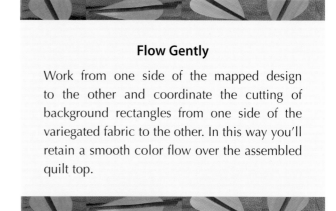

Flow Gently

Work from one side of the mapped design to the other and coordinate the cutting of background rectangles from one side of the variegated fabric to the other. In this way you'll retain a smooth color flow over the assembled quilt top.

2. From the grayish brown background fabric, cut a rectangle along the straight of grain that is 1¼" larger on all sides than the finished block should be. In this case, for a finished block 5½" x 5¾", cut out an 8" x 8¼" rectangle of background fabric.

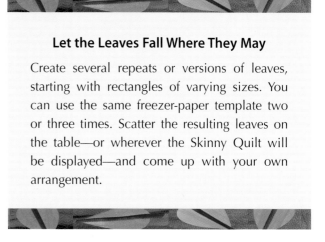

Let the Leaves Fall Where They May

Create several repeats or versions of leaves, starting with rectangles of varying sizes. You can use the same freezer-paper template two or three times. Scatter the resulting leaves on the table—or wherever the Skinny Quilt will be displayed—and come up with your own arrangement.

3. Follow steps 1–10 of "Leaf Samples" to piece each block.

assembling the skinny quilt

1. If you're following the pattern arrangement for the featured quilt, arrange the blocks as shown at right. Fill in with pieces of background fabric, cut ¼" larger on each side for seam allowances. Stitch the blocks in each section together. Sew the sections together in numerical order.

   If you're creating your own layout, arrange the blocks on a design wall or large, flat surface. Strive for easy assembly with a minimum of set-in pieces by aligning blocks and adding plain pieces of background fabric where needed to even out the section. Whenever possible, stitch blocks together into units, and then stitch units together.

2. Trim the edges of the pieced center so they are even and square.

3. Measure the length of the quilt top through the center and cut two 4"-wide strips from the background/border fabric. Sew the strips together end to end to make one long strip and then trim the strip to the length needed. Repeat to make one additional border strip. Sew the strips to the sides of the quilt top. Press the seam allowances toward the border strips. Repeat to cut and sew borders to the top and bottom edges of the quilt top.

quilting and finishing

Refer to "Quiltmaking Basics and More" on page 89 as needed.

1. Press the quilt top. Layer the backing, batting, and quilt top; baste.

2. Quilt with threads to match the fabrics. First, as an extra precaution to keep the layers from shifting, use a walking foot to stitch in the ditch around the border and in the seams between blocks.

3. Using a darning foot, free-motion quilt the background fabric in each block and border strip. Notice Frieda's wood-grain pattern in the photo on page 52.

4. Trim the backing and batting even with the quilt top. Use the goldish brown batik 2½"-wide strips to make and attach a double-fold binding.

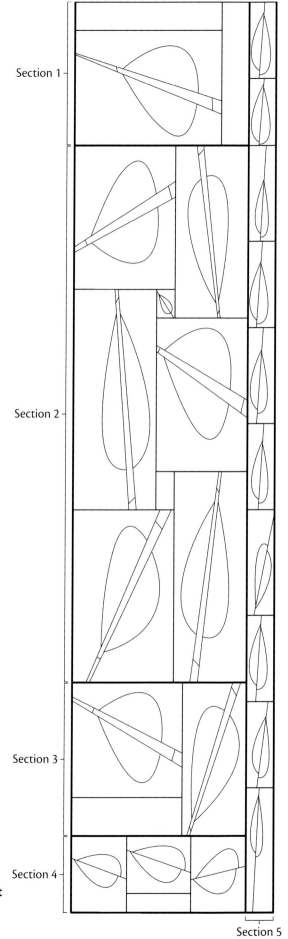

Section 1

Section 2

Section 3

Section 4

Section 5

"Blushing Aspens" block patterns and block arrangement
Enlarge 500%.

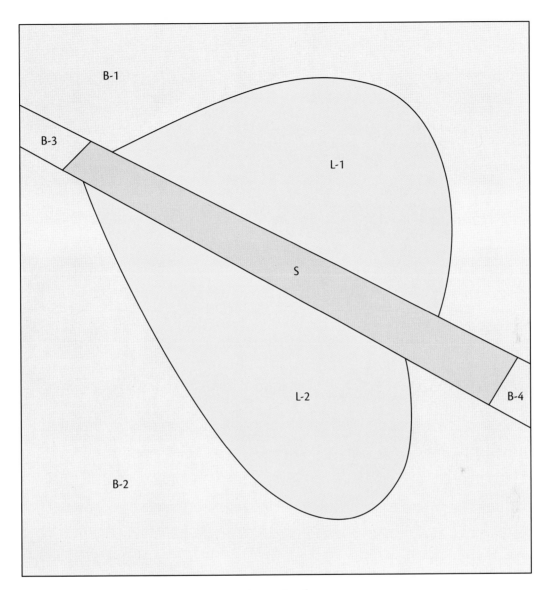

Large Leaf

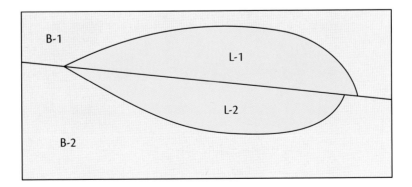

Small Leaf

rhubarb crisp RUNNER *by Jo Morton*

The best way of "preserving our ties to the past," according to Jo Morton, is making "new quilts that look old." She shows the way back in time with reproduction fabrics—many of them her own designs—and with classic Sawtooth Star blocks, framed by flying-geese sashing. The small-scale (but not miniature!) blocks are combined using Jo's clever and precise method. Loaded with old-fashioned charm, this runner is a skinny version of an earlier quilt design called Rhubarb Crisp. Like the forerunner, this runner brings to mind the dessert savored on the nineteenth-century homestead. You can practically smell the flavorful rhubarb baked with sugar and spice!

Running low on time? Simple stitch-in-the-ditch and X-marks-the-spot machine quilting lets you finish at warp speed. But this is the perfect carry-along project for hand quilting should anyone care to linger in the needle-art joys of our great-grandmothers!

Pieced by Mary Fornoff; machine quilted by Bonnie Haith; bound by Sheri Dowding

Finished measurements: 14" x 38"

materials

Fabrics are 100%-cotton reproduction fabrics. Yardages are based on fabrics that measure 42" wide.

Scraps of 12 light neutral prints with tan, ecru, taupe, or gold as the background color for Sawtooth Star blocks

Scraps of 12 medium to dark prints with rust, brown, and black predominating for Sawtooth Star blocks

Scraps of 4 to 8 additional light prints and 4 to 8 additional dark prints for flying-geese sashing

7½" x 10" piece *each* of 2 different reddish brown prints for cornerstones

¼ yard of brown print for binding

¾ yard of fabric for backing

18" x 42" piece of batting

cutting

Cut all strips on the crosswise grain (selvage to selvage). Trim selvages.

From the dark prints for flying-geese sashing, cut:
32 sets of 4 matching squares, 1⅞" x 1⅞" (128 total)

From the light prints for flying-geese sashing, cut a *total* of:
32 squares, 3¼" x 3¼"

From *each* of the 12 light neutral prints for blocks, cut:
1 square, 3¼" x 3¼" (12 total)
4 squares, 1½" x 1½" (48 total)

From *each* of the 12 medium to dark prints for blocks, cut:
1 square, 2½" x 2½" (12 total)
4 squares, 1⅞" x 1⅞" (48 total)

From *each* of the 2 different reddish brown prints, cut:
12 squares, 2½" x 2½" (24 total; you will have 3 left over)

From the brown print, cut:
3 strips, 1¼" x 42"

making the flying-geese units

1. Draw a diagonal line on the wrong side of four matching dark 1⅞" squares.

2. Align two of these squares on opposite corners of a light 3¼" square, right sides together. The squares will overlap in the center and the drawn lines will connect. Sew ¼" from both sides of the drawn line. Cut apart on the drawn line. Press the seam allowances toward the small triangles.

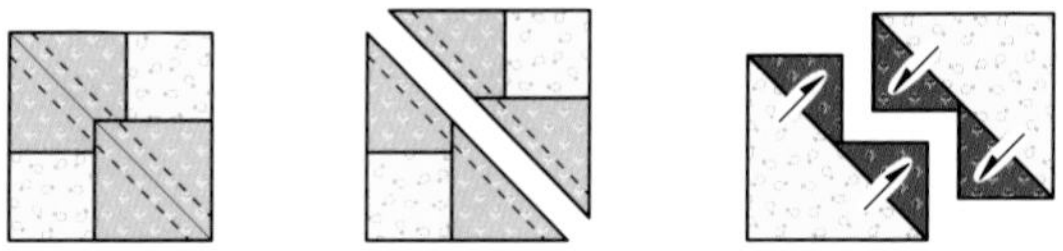

3. Place a dark 1⅞" square on top of the large triangle of each unit from step 2, aligning the left side and bottom edges. Make sure the drawn diagonal line starts at the corner and ends at the center. Sew ¼" from both sides of the drawn line. Cut apart on the drawn line. Press the seam allowances toward the dark triangles. Each unit will make two flying-geese units for a total of four matching units. If necessary, trim each unit to measure 1½" x 2½".

4. Repeat steps 1–3 with the remaining light and dark pieces for flying-geese units to make a total of 128 units.

5. Sew four different flying-geese units together along the long edges. Repeat to make a total of 32 flying-geese sashing units.

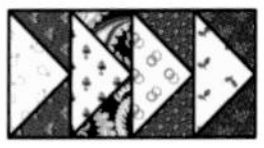

Make 32.

making the sawtooth star blocks

1. Refer to steps 1–3 above to make 12 sets of four matching flying-geese units using the light 3¼" squares and dark 1⅞" squares cut for the blocks.

2. Arrange four matching flying-geese units, the matching dark 2½" square, and the four matching light 1½" squares in three horizontal rows. Sew the pieces in each row together; press the seam allowances toward the squares. Sew the rows together, nesting the seam allowances; press the seam allowances toward the center row. Repeat to make a total of 12 Sawtooth Star blocks.

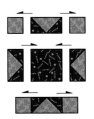

Make 12.

Jo's Clip Trick

For a Sawtooth Star block that lies flat, on either side of the nested seam allowances, cut through both layers of the seam allowance, right up to the stitching. Press the flying-geese unit seam allowances toward the center and the corner square allowances outward. Press the seam allowance intersections open.

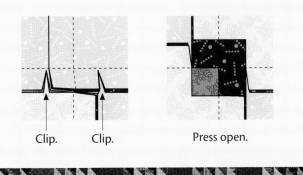

Clip.   Clip.   Press open.

assembling the skinny quilt top

1. Refer to the photo on page 59 to arrange the Sawtooth Star blocks in two rows of six blocks each, leaving plenty of space between each block. Strive for a pleasing balance of colors. Place a flying-geese sashing unit on each side of each block, paying careful attention to the direction of the points. Fill in with the reddish brown 2½" squares. For the quilt shown, the same print was used for the squares for the center three horizontal rows and a different print was used for the squares in the two horizontal rows on each end. Reposition sashing strips as needed so the color distribution is well balanced.

2. When you're satisfied with the arrangement, pin and sew the pieces in each row together. Gently press the seam allowances toward the blocks or cornerstones; avoid stretching the sashing strips.

3. Pin and sew the rows together, matching seam intersections. Use Jo's Clip Trick at left at the seam intersections. Press sashing strip seam allowances toward the block or cornerstone.

quilting and finishing

Refer to "Quiltmaking Basics and More" on page 89 as needed.

1. Cut the backing fabric in half lengthwise, remove the selvages, and sew the two pieces together end to end; press. Press the quilt top. Layer the backing, batting, and quilt top; baste.

2. Quilt as desired or as follows. Stitch in the ditch of all seams, and stitch diagonally in both directions over the Sawtooth Star block centers and cornerstones.

3. Trim the quilt batting and backing even with the edges of the quilt top. Use the brown print 1¼"-wide strips to make and attach a single-fold binding.

Antique quilts are a major source of design ideas for Joanna Figueroa of Fig Tree & Co., along with vintage fabric swatches and wrapping paper, children's illustrations from the early 1900s, and flea market finds. Whether it's a fabric collection or a quilt, Joanna always starts with the colors—often a fresh, romantic palette. This explains the classic House blocks, the simple one-patch mosaic, combined with the fresh look of soft pastel prints and surprising touches of wool in the Oak Leaf and Reel appliqué.

Pieced by Valerie Marsh and Joanna Figueroa; quilted by Diana Johnson

Finished measurements: 19" x 70"

materials

Fabrics are 100% cotton, unless otherwise indicated. Yardages for cotton are based on fabrics that measure 42" wide; yardages for wool are based on fabrics that measure at least 36" wide after felting.

¼ yard *each* of 6 different brown or terra-cotta prints for House blocks

1 yard *total* of assorted cream, ivory, and light tan prints for background squares

⅜ yard of cream print for House blocks

½ yard of pale yellow print for border

¼ yard of light khaki or tan felted wool for oak leaf appliqués

¼ yard of orange print for reel appliqués

Scraps of rose felted wool for berry appliqués

½ yard of green print for binding

2¼ yards of fabric for backing

23" x 74" piece of batting

Threads to match appliqué fabrics

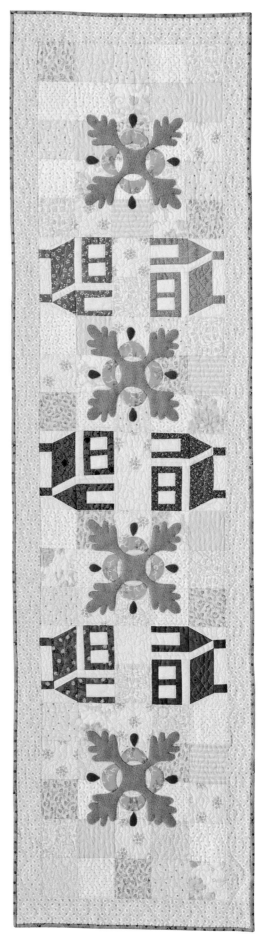

cutting

Cut all strips on the crosswise grain of the fabric (selvage to selvage). Trim selvages. Patterns for pieces N, O, and P are on page 68. As you cut, label each stack with a lettered sticker.

From the cream print for House blocks, cut:
2 strips, 1½" x 42"; crosscut into:

    12 squares, 1½" x 1½" (A)

    6 rectangles, 1½" x 3¼" (B)

    6 rectangles, 1½" x 2¾" (C)

    12 rectangles, 1½" x 1⅞" (D)

2 strips, 1⅛" x 42"; crosscut into:

    6 rectangles, 1⅛" x 3½" (E)

    6 rectangles, 1⅛" x 3⅞" (F)

1 strip, 1¹/₁₆" x 42"; crosscut into 6 rectangles, 1¹/₁₆" x 4" (G)*

6 pattern N pieces

6 pattern N reversed pieces

*Cut your strip width a smidgen over 1" but less than 1⅛". This way your diagonal roof pieces will better match the house pieces.

From *each* of the 6 brown or terra-cotta prints, cut:
1 rectangle, 1¼" x 2½" (H)

2 rectangles, 1" x 2¾" (I)

2 rectangles, 1" x 3⅞" (J)

2 rectangles, 1" x 1⅞" (K)

2 rectangles, 1⅛" x 1½" (L)

1 rectangle, ⅞" x 1⅞" (M)

1 pattern O piece

1 pattern P piece

From the assorted cream, ivory, and light tan prints, cut a *total* of:
86 squares, 3½" x 3½"

From the pale yellow print, cut:
5 strips, 2½" x 42"

From the green print, cut:
5 strips, 2¼" x 42"

making the house blocks

In general, press seam allowances toward the terra-cotta piece. If the instructions specify pressing toward the cream fabric, trim ⅛" from the terra-cotta seam allowance to prevent any shadowing through.

1. Arrange the terra-cotta and cream pieces for one block into three sections as shown. All the terra-cotta pieces should be the same fabric and all the cream pieces should be the same fabric.

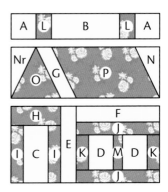

2. For the chimney section, sew the A, B, and L pieces together as shown. Press the seam allowances toward the L pieces.

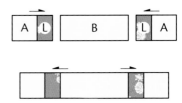

3. For the roof section, center and sew the G piece to the right edge of the O piece (G is longer than necessary). Press the seam allowances toward the G piece. Trim the ends of the G piece even with the point and the lower edge of the O piece as shown.

4. Add the P piece to the right edge of the G piece. Position the P piece so that it extends ¼" above the G piece at the upper edge. Press the seam allowances toward the P piece. Trim the dog-ears.

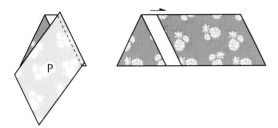

A Good Roofing Job!

When joining two pieces with diagonal edges, always offset the pieces by ¼" so that the edges of the finished unit will be aligned.

5. Add the N piece to the right edge of the unit from step 4, and the N reversed piece to the left edge, offsetting the pieces as before. Press the seam allowances toward the N pieces, and trim the dog-ears.

6. For the door and windows section, begin by sewing C between two I pieces. Press the seam allowances toward the I pieces. Sew an H piece on top. Add an E piece to the right side of this unit.

   Sew the K, D, and M pieces together as shown. Press the seam allowances toward the K and M pieces. Stitch a J piece above and below this unit, and an F piece above that; press. Stitch the doorway unit to the window unit. Press the seam allowances toward the E piece.

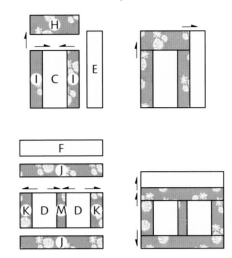

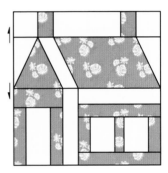

7. Stitch the three sections together; press as indicated. Trim the finished block to 6½" square.

8. Repeat steps 1–7 to make a total of six House blocks.

Inspiration from Afar

Joanna used traditional American motifs to interpret a place she discovered abroad while on vacation. "On one of the two islands that lie in the middle of the river Seine, there is a little place, seemingly untouched by time," she relates. "It feels like a tiny forgotten village right in the middle of bustling, metropolitan Paris." Which just goes to prove, you can capture the feeling of home anywhere at all—and stitch it into a quilt. A more perfect housewarming gift you won't find anywhere in the world!

making the appliquéd sections

1. Randomly select 25 assorted cream, ivory, and light tan print 3½" squares and arrange them in five rows of five squares each. Sew the squares in each row together. Press the seam allowances in opposite directions from row to row. Sew the rows together. Press the seam allowances out from the center row. Repeat to make a total of two sections.

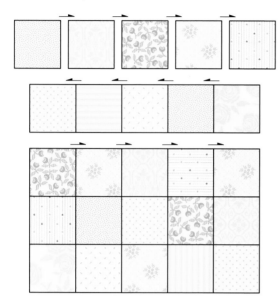

Make 2.

2. Repeat step 1 with 15 squares, arranging them in five rows of three squares each. Make a total of two sections.

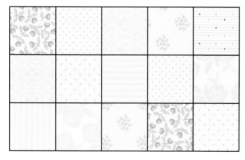

Make 2.

3. Sew the remaining squares into three pairs.

4. Use the patterns on page 69 to make the appliqués. To make the oak leaf template, fold an 8" square of freezer paper into quarters. Unfold and align the creases with the dash lines on the pattern, dull side up; trace the pattern onto one quarter of the paper. Refold, cut along the traced lines, and then unfold the complete template. Press this piece onto the khaki or tan wool and cut out along the template edges. Peel off the freezer paper and use the template repeatedly to cut a total of four oak leaf motifs.

   Trace several berry shapes onto the dull side of the freezer paper and use the templates to cut out 16 motifs from the rose wool, reusing each template until it no longer adheres to the fabric when pressed.

   Trace the reel pattern onto freezer paper four times; cut out the templates. Press the templates onto the right side of the orange print. Cut out each shape, adding ¼" around each one. Spray some starch into a dish. Working on one reel shape at a time, use a small paintbrush or cotton swab to apply the liquid starch to the wrong side of the seam allowance. Press the seam allowance over the freezer-paper edge, clipping into seam allowances sparingly to create smooth edges. Carefully remove the freezer paper and press the shape lightly. Repeat with the remaining three reel pieces.

5. Referring to the photo on page 63 as needed, center a reel shape on each of the 3 x 5 patchwork sections from step 2. Temporarily secure the pieces with dots of glue stick, fabric glue, or silk pins. Use matching thread to appliqué the pieces in place. Next, center an oak leaf shape over each reel. Use matching thread and whipstitch along the edges. Because you are stitching on wool, you will need to take somewhat larger stitches. Finally, add a berry to each side of the reel. Repeat the appliqué process on each of the 5 x 5 patchwork sections from step 1, but center the design on the seam of the second horizontal row, rather than the exact center.

assembling the skinny quilt top

1. Lay out the appliquéd patchwork sections, the patchwork pairs, and the House blocks as shown. Sew the House blocks and patchwork pairs together. Press the seam allowances toward the squares. Sew the sections together; press the seam allowances toward the house units.

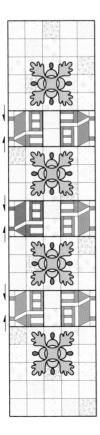

2. Sew two pale yellow strips together to make one long strip. Repeat with two more strips. Measure the long edges of the quilt and trim the strips to this measurement. Sew the strips to the sides of the quilt top. Press the seam allowances toward the borders. Cut the remaining pale yellow strip in half crosswise. Measure the short ends of the quilt and trim the half strips to this measurement. Sew the strips to the ends of the quilt. Press the seam allowances toward the border.

quilting and finishing

Refer to "Quiltmaking Basics and More" on page 89 as needed.

1. Press the quilt top. Layer the backing, batting, and quilt top; baste.

2. Machine quilt 1/16" from the seams in each House block. Free-motion quilt a clamshell or feather design over the roof and outline the elements of each oak leaf, berry, and reel shape. Work a small meandering stitch over the patchwork background and in the cream fabrics of the house chimney and roof sections. Sew a swirly linear pattern along the border strips.

3. Trim the batting and backing even with the edges of the quilt top. Use the green 2¼"-wide strips to make and attach a double-fold binding.

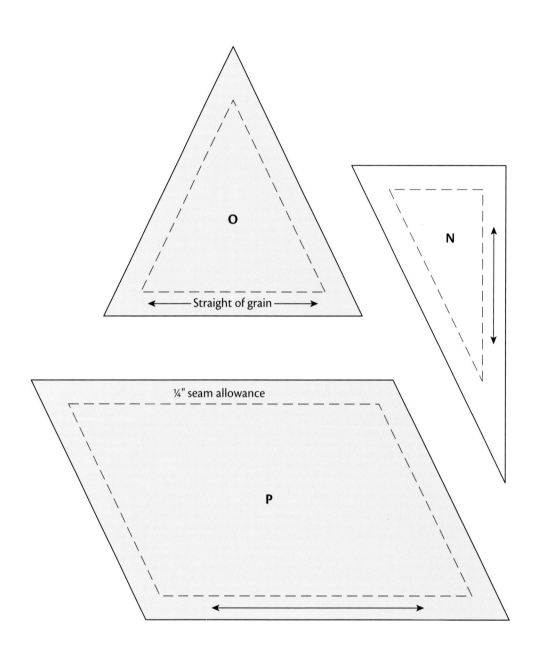

O

Straight of grain

N

¼" seam allowance

P

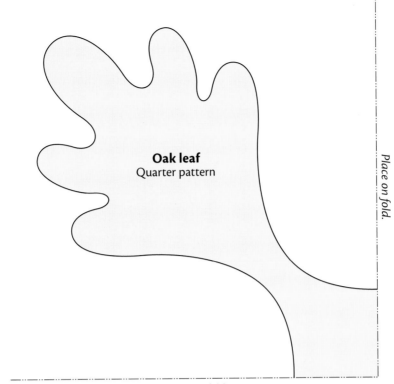

Oak leaf
Quarter pattern

Place on fold.

Place on fold.

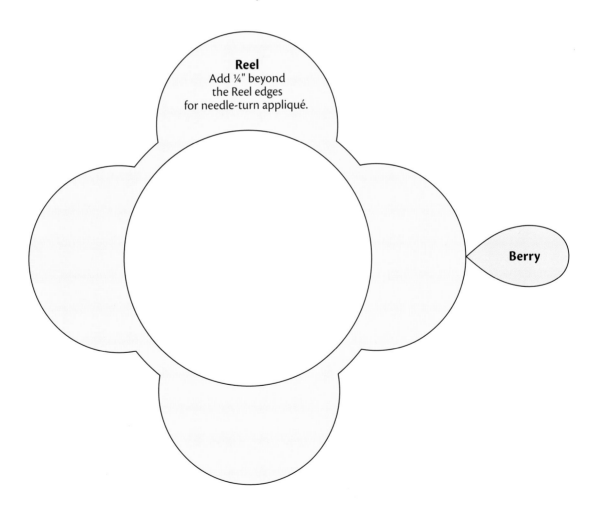

Reel
Add ¼" beyond
the Reel edges
for needle-turn appliqué.

Berry

wisteria LANE *by Melinda Bula*

"A purple wisteria was the first plant I put in my garden," says Melinda Bula, reminiscing about the time when her dream house became a reality. She trained the clustered blooms to run up brick pillars... and replicated the beautiful results on her Skinny Quilt. Of course, white flowers with pinkish overtones would look equally lush. According to the Victorian language of flowers, wisteria translates to "I cling to thee," so the delicate florals and sturdy bricks—the object being clung to—provide a highly romantic combination! Cultivated with fusible, raw-edged appliqué and lavish free-motion quilting, wisteria joins the many varieties that can be found in Melinda's *Cutting Garden Quilts*. Wouldn't this design look positively di-vine clinging to *your* table or walls?

Finished measurements: 17" x 72"

materials

In addition to the materials listed below, you will also need the fabrics listed in the fabric key on page 72. Fabrics are 100%-cotton mottled solids or hand-dyed fabrics so that different shades of a color can be fussy cut from different areas of the same piece of fabric. Yardages are based on fabrics that measure 42" wide. Fat quarters (18" x 21") can be substituted for ¼-yard cuts; fat eighths (9" x 21") can be substituted for ⅛-yard cuts.

2¼ yards of fabric for backing

21" x 76" rectangle of low-loft cotton batting

6 yards of 18"-wide repositionable fusible web such as Steam-A-Seam 2 Double Stick (see "Resources" on page 94)

30-weight rayon thread in lavender, variegated green, brown, ecru, and maroon to match flowers, leaves, and background

Tracing paper or freezer paper

Chalk pencil

fabric key

A ■ 2⅝ yards (background and binding)

B ■ ½ yard

C ■ ¼ yard

D ■ ½ yard

E ▢ ½ yard

F ▢ ¼ yard

G ▢ ½ yard

H ■ ¼ yard

I ▢ ½ yard

J ▢ ¼ yard

K ▢ ½ yard

L ▢ ¼ yard

M ▢ ⅛ yard

N ▢ ⅛ yard

O ▢ ⅛ yard

cutting

From the *lengthwise grain* of fabric A, cut:

1 piece, 17" x 72"

3 strips, 2" x length of fabric

making the brick wall background

1. Referring to "Fusible Appliqué the Easy Way" on page 90 and following the manufacturer's instructions, apply the fusible web to the wrong sides of all the fabrics except for the background and binding fabric and the backing fabric.

2. Lay out the fabric A 17" x 72" piece on a flat surface. To make the bricks, cut 32 rectangles, roughly 2" x 5", from fabric B. Cut 30 strips, ½" x 18", from fabric C for the mortar.

3. Starting 6" from the top of the background piece and cutting some bricks crosswise in half, arrange the brick and mortar pieces in a staggered pattern. You do not need to cover the entire background; the flowers will conceal much of this pattern. Stop about 6" from the bottom. Press lightly with an iron.

adding the vines and stems

1. Using a rotary cutter but no ruler, cut five free-form curvy lines across the entire width of fabric D, keeping lines at least ½" apart. Making them choppy and wiggly is a good thing, because they will more closely simulate a rough, twiggy vine.

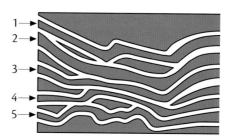

2. Beginning 6" from the ends of the background, refer to the vine and stem placement diagram below right to randomly position vines along the lengthwise center of the brick wall. Cut one or two vines apart and arrange offshoots radiating out to the sides.

3. Trace the wisteria stem pattern on page 75 onto tracing paper or freezer paper; cut it out. Pin it to the right side of fabric E and then cut out the shape. Reuse the pattern to cut out 11 stems. Reverse the pattern and cut out four more stems for a total of 15 stems.

4. Using a chalk pencil, mark across the width of the background at 12" intervals. This grid will help you with placement of stems and flowers.

5. Position the stems on the background, beginning at a vine and changing direction often.

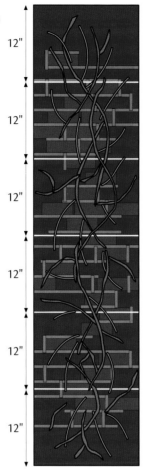

12"
12"
12"
12"
12"
12"
12"

Vine and stem placement

adding the flowers, leaves, and tendrils

1. Photocopy the wisteria pattern on page 75 three time—once to keep the pattern intact for reference and twice more for cutting; some pattern pieces overlap. Cut apart the two patterns designated for cutting so you have one each of petal shapes 1–32.

Calling All Adventurous Gardeners!

Why not cut all the shapes freehand? Use the pattern merely as a visual guide and cut shapes that are similar in size and shape. Because no two flowers are exactly alike, and you're striving for an organic look, it's impossible to fail at growing a beautiful wisteria vine!

2. Cut and assemble one wisteria cluster at a time. For a dimensional, varied, and realistic look, each cluster should include three fabric shades: light, medium, and dark, and varying sizes of petals. Refer to the shaded tones in the pattern. As you use the patterns to cut out the shapes from fabric with repositionable fusible web on the back, stick them to a stem. Begin with the lavender flowers, and then make the blue flowers, and end with the pink flowers. Refer to the photo on page 71 and the chart below to cut each flower piece from the suggested fabric.

Start by folding fusible-backed fabric in half or accordion fold in thirds and fourths. Working in numerical order, pin a pattern piece on top, and scissor cut through all layers (the pieces are numbered so that the light-value pieces are cut first, the medium-value pieces next, and the darkest pieces last). This will speed up the process and give you mirror images of flowers for left and right sides of the wisteria. You can always trim or individualize some of the flowers cut this way. In spite of the fact that there is just one pattern, each of your wisteria clusters should be slightly different. As you cut out each piece, stick it in place.

FLOWER COLOR	NUMBER OF EACH PIECE TO CUT	FABRIC FOR PIECES 1–13	FABRIC FOR PIECES 14–22	FABRIC FOR PIECES 23–32
Lavender	8	H	G	O
Blue	5	J	I	O
Pink	2	K	G	L

3. Using the leaf patterns on page 75, follow the same process for making the leaf templates as you did for previous pieces. Start by making 12 stems from a variety of your green fabrics. Cut 100 leaves from fabrics E and F. Accordion fold fabrics to cut out more than one leaf at a time and to make some leaves mirror images. Cut some of the leaves freehand to vary the sizes and shapes.

4. Add groups of stems and leaves in clusters around the wisteria. Also, fill in randomly with single leaves wherever you feel they ought to be. Cover the background lushly, yet still allow some of the bricks and mortar to show through the foliage. Refer to the photo and the flower and leaf placement diagram as needed.

5. Referring to the leaf patterns, cut smaller leaf shapes from fabrics E, F, M, and N, and place these pieces on top of contrasting-color leaves for highlights.

6. Use the tendril pattern on page 75 to cut five pieces from fabric M, varying some of the shapes and cutting others as mirror images. Position the tendrils, well spaced, on the quilt top. Cut away some sections of the tendrils so they appear to wrap around a vine.

7. Take time to rearrange the flower, leaf, and tendril pieces so the composition looks organic, well balanced, and varied. Add more accents and highlights to areas that seem a little dull. When you're satisfied with the entire arrangement, press the quilt top with a hot iron.

Flower, leaf, and tendril placement

Introduce the Unexpected!

Add the lively quirks that only happen in nature: an occasional purple accent on a mauve wisteria or a periwinkle blue flower as part of a lavender cluster.

finishing

Refer to "Quiltmaking Basics and More" on page 89 as needed.

1. Layer the backing, batting, and quilt top; baste.

2. Free-motion quilt the top, working outward from the center. Using lavender thread, free-motion quilt all the flowers, stitching on the edges of each flower petal and echoing the shape once or twice more inside of the first outline. With variegated green thread, stitch over the edges of each stem and leaf and add veins.

3. Add a tendril or two with free-motion quilting in ecru, wherever you would like a light accent. Use brown thread to stitch along the edges of each mortar piece that shows, and maroon thread to work concentric echo patterns over the bricks and dark red background.

4. Press the quilt. Trim the backing and batting even with the quilt top. Use the 2"-wide strips of fabric A to make and attach a single-fold binding.

Flower stem and petals

1
4
31
5
2
15
3
6
14
7
8
9
16
32
11
23
24
10
25
26
13
27
12
28
17
18
29
19
22
20
30
21

Leaves and stem

Tendril

WAKING UP, down the shore *by Eleanor Levie*

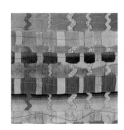

Yours truly, this book's editor, loves to sleep in, given half a chance. But when I'm on a summer vacation seaside in New Jersey (or, as the locals say, "down the shore"), I can't wait to get up and catch the sunrise over the Atlantic. And now I've captured the scene, calling upon my crafty side, some pretty, variegated fabrics, and a stash of ribbons and rickrack. Find out how easy and fun it is to play with ribbons in different ways. First, weave ribbons—just like making those loopy potholders when we were young! Second, couch sheer ribbons to spread an ethereal sky into your landscape . . . and quilt your project at the same time. And finally, make just three folds in a strand of grosgrain ribbon to form a seagull in flight. Even in the dead of winter, you'll enjoy the view from a long, narrow "window," conjuring up the feeling of being at some wonderfully warm and relaxing get-away spot.

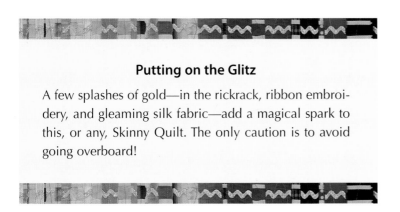

Putting on the Glitz

A few splashes of gold—in the rickrack, ribbon embroidery, and gleaming silk fabric—add a magical spark to this, or any, Skinny Quilt. The only caution is to avoid going overboard!

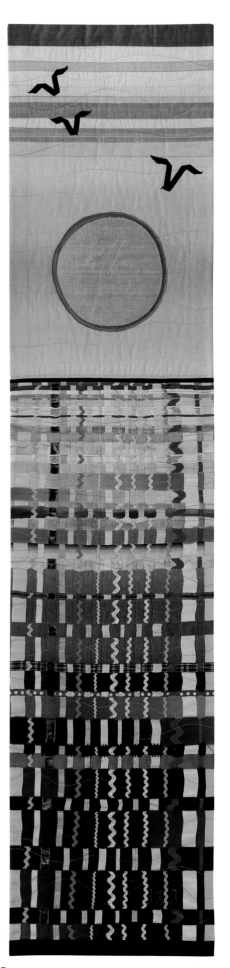

Finished measurements: 14" x 60"

materials

Unless otherwise indicated, fabrics are 100% cotton. Variegated fabrics are Gradations by Caryl Bryer Fallert for Benartex (see "Resources" on page 94 for this fabric as well as silk dupioni). Yardages are based on fabrics that measure 42" wide. Avoid 100%-nylon ribbons and trims because they will melt under the heat of the iron.

Variegated fabrics: ½ yard of Sunset #37 (peach to yellow) for sky; ⅛ yard *each* of Blue Topaz #5 (lavender to light blue), Ultra Blue #50 (light to medium blue), and Navy #58 (medium blue to midnight blue) for water

1 fat quarter *each* of R44 (golden yellow) and Violet silk dupioni

2 yards of fabric for backing and facings

1⅛ yards *each* of 8 to 10 metallic gold, gold, yellow, aqua, light blue, and medium blue rickrack in assorted widths

1⅛ yards *each* of black, blue, metallic gold, seafoam, light blue, lavender, purple, variegated blues, and blue with white polka-dot grosgrain ribbon in assorted widths up to 1"

1⅛ yards *each* of yellow, seafoam, turquoise, aqua, blue, and purple single- or double-faced satin ribbon in assorted widths up to 1"

1⅛ yards *each* of blue, pink, yellow, green, and lavender hand-dyed silk ribbons in assorted widths from ⅝"

1⅛ yards *each* of blue, black, turquoise, and white novelty ribbons and trims, such as velvet, braided, picot edges, and flat braid in assorted widths

½ yard *each* of pearlescent white, pink, rose, and lavender sheer ribbons in widths from ⅝" to 1¼"

⅝ yard of ⅜"-wide black grosgrain ribbon for seagulls

½ yard of black grosgrain ribbon at least 1⅜" wide for bottom border facing

18" x 64" piece of batting

1¼ yards of 17"-wide heavyweight paper-backed fusible web

¼ yard of 17"-wide lightweight paper-backed fusible web

¼"-wide double-stick fusible tape such as Steam-A-Seam

Variegated blue-to-white rayon thread and variegated peach rayon thread for quilting

Basting spray

cutting

From the variegated peach to yellow fabric, cut:
1 piece, 18" x 25"

From the fabric for backing, cut:
1 piece, 18" x 64"
2 strips, 2" x 64"

From the violet silk dupioni, cut:
1 strip, 5" x 18"

weaving the water section

1. Place the heavyweight fusible web, paper side down, on a large padded surface suitable for ironing and one that you can pin into. Pin down the web at each corner.

2. Evenly space 21 assorted ribbons and trims lengthwise to the fusible web to create the warp strands for weaving. Extend each length slightly beyond the fusible web and pin at the top and bottom so the lengths are taut. Begin with an assortment of gold and yellow rickracks and ribbons in the center and then add light blues and blue-green ribbons across the remaining width. Use a length of duct tape to secure the ribbons across the

extended edges at the top; keep the pins at the bottom. This way, you'll be able to lift lengths as needed to weave.

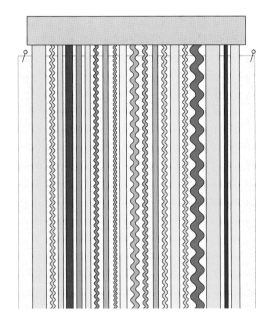

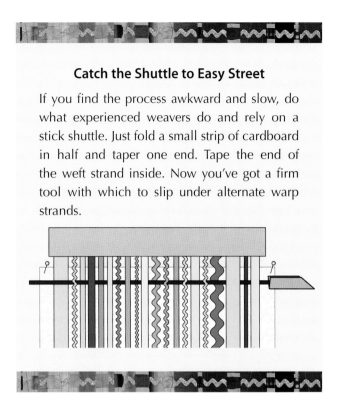

Catch the Shuttle to Easy Street

If you find the process awkward and slow, do what experienced weavers do and rely on a stick shuttle. Just fold a small strip of cardboard in half and taper one end. Tape the end of the weft strand inside. Now you've got a firm tool with which to slip under alternate warp strands.

3. Set aside the sheer ribbons, the 3/8"-wide black grosgrain ribbon, the black grosgrain ribbon for the bottom facing, and one narrow black and one narrow gold ribbon for use later. The remaining ribbons and trims will be used as the horizontal weaving strands, known as the weft. Begin at the end that will be closest to the sky piece with 1/16"- and 1/8"-wide ribbons. Choose a dark-colored ribbon and weave it under the first warp, over the next, and under the next. Continue this under-and-over pattern across the width. To make the weaving process easier, you may want to thread the ribbon onto a large-eyed tapestry needle and use it to guide the ribbon under alternate warps. Then, trim the ribbon so it extends 1" beyond the fusible web at both sides, and move it up to within 1/2" of the end of the piece; pin down the ends.

   Weave a second ribbon so it passes over the first warp, under the second, and so on all the way across. Slide it up close to the first weft strand, then trim the excess and secure the ends with pins. Switching to pale-colored, but still narrow ribbons, continue weaving in this way for 3", pushing each ribbon up close to the previous one as you finish weaving it.

4. Introduce strips of variegated blue fabrics as weft strands. By tearing these strips, you'll get extra texture for your weaving. Near the horizon, use narrow, pale light blue and lavender strips, 1/2" wide and 18" long. Intersperse pale-colored ribbons, 1/4" to 5/8" wide, in the weaving. Continue to push each successive weft up close to the one before, to completely conceal the fusible web underneath. Weave in this way for another 9".

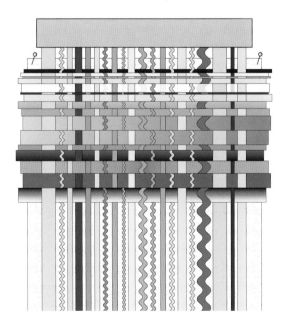

5. Gradually change weft strands as follows: choose a medium range of blues that become dark navy and black. Choose wider and wider ribbons, trims, and torn fabric strips, ranging up to 2½" wide. Occasionally weave in an unusual ribbon, such as a narrower velvet or plaid. Continue until the sheet of fusible web is completely covered.

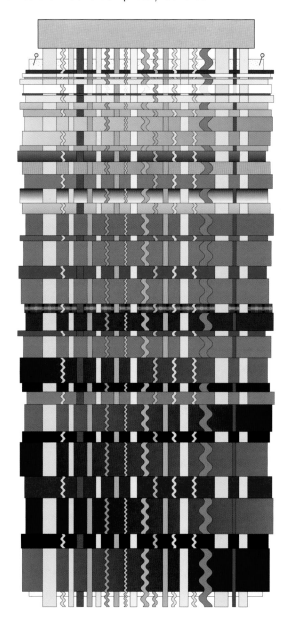

6. Assess your woven cloth. If there is a warp or weft strand that seems to stand out too much, substitute another choice. To do this, attach one end of the new strand to one end of the old using a small pin or safety pin. Pull the opposite end of the strand you wish to replace, guiding the new strand in to take its place.

7. At the top of the piece, or horizon, remove the duct tape and insert a ½" strip of blue fabric in the open area. Then, fuse your woven cloth from the front, following the manufacturer's instructions, and going over every area of the weaving with the iron. Be sure to use a nonstick pressing sheet over the ribbons to protect synthetics. Turn the piece over and fuse from the back. Let the piece cool, and then peel off the paper backing.

assembling the skinny quilt

1. With right sides together, align the peach edge of the variegated peach-to-yellow piece at the top of the woven piece. Sew, using a ¼" seam allowance. Finger-press the seam allowances toward the woven piece.

2. Using the basting spray, baste the backing piece, batting, and quilt top together, following the manufacturer's instructions. Using a pressing sheet, press the quilt from the front, moving from the horizon outward, and to both ends. Press from the back as well. Trim the Skinny Quilt to measure 15" x 62".

3. Finger-press fusible tape to the long edges of the sheer ribbons. Making sure they are parallel with the top edge, adhere them across the sky fabric, between 3" and 9" from the top edge, as shown in the photograph on page 77. Allow some strands to overlap others. Using a pressing cloth and an iron set on low, tack them in place.

4. To make the sun, refer to "Circling Around" on page 92 and draw three 7"-diameter circles onto the paper side of the lightweight fusible web. Roughly cut out the circles. Fuse one circle to the wrong side of the golden yellow silk dupioni; fuse another circle to a scrap of batting. Cut out these circles along the marked lines. Press the third circle onto the wrong side of the violet silk dupioni. Cut it out ¼" beyond the marked line on the fusible web. Peel the paper backing from each circle.

With the fusible side down, center the batting on the sky. Center the golden yellow circle on top of the violet circle. Using matching thread, stitch several times around the edges of the yellow circle. Center these layered silk circles over the batting circle and fuse in place. Using thread to match, stitch several times around the edges of the violet circle.

5. Using variegated blue-to-white rayon thread, stitch across each weft strand. Keep the lines of stitching fairly straight down the center of the narrow strands near the horizon, becoming gradually more wavy, randomly swooping from one side to the other along the wider strands. Pin the narrow black ribbon and the narrow gold ribbon over the horizon seam and couch over them to further emphasize the horizon.

Don't Get Caught!

To prevent the presser foot from catching on all the loose ribbons and trims, try the following techniques: Use a wide, blunt-end presser foot, such as an appliqué or couching foot. Engage the needle-down function. Stitch slowly. Stretch warp ribbons out flat and taut as you come to them or use a stiletto to keep strands flat. If the presser foot goes under a ribbon, stop stitching, raise the presser foot, and push the ribbon under the foot.

6. Using variegated peach thread, quilt wavy lines along the sky and the sheer ribbons in the sky section. Also, stitch down the edges of the sheer ribbons.

finishing

Refer to "Quiltmaking Basics and More" on page 89 as needed.

1. Trim and square up the quilt.

2. To make the ribbon seagulls, cut the ³/₈"-wide black grosgrain ribbon into one 8" strand and two 7" strands. For each bird, fold the center at a 45° angle to form a V. Pin to the desired position on the sky. Fold each end under at a 90° angle, and pin. Use small, sharp scissors to cut each end at an angle. Free-motion quilt each seagull with black thread, adding a curve to the wing tips and a beak at the bottom fold, if desired.

Free-motion quilt wing tips and beak.

3. Add facings to each side and press ¼" to the wrong side on one long end of the 2" x 64" strips of backing fabric. Pin the opposite edge to each long side of the quilt, right sides together and raw edges even; stitch. Press to set the seam, and then fold the facings to the back, so that no part of it shows on the front of the quilt. Press, using a presser sheet. Pin the folded edge to the backing and slip-stitch it in place.

4. Add a hanging sleeve and bottom rod casing to the back and stitch to the top and bottom edges through all layers.

5. Center the violet silk strip on the top edge of the quilt, with right sides together. Stitch 1½" from the top edge. Fold the violet strip up. Fold the sides of the strip over onto the back to meet but not overlap the hanging sleeve; hem and slip-stitch the edges in place. Then, fold the violet strip over the top to the backing. Fold the long edge under ½"; pin it to the hanging sleeve and slip-stitch in place. Cut a 16" length from the wide black grosgrain ribbon that you set aside earlier. Use it to finish the bottom edge in a similar way, but without hemming the woven edge on the back.

Like all the masterpieces in Sue Benner's Flower series, this Skinny Quilt celebrates the radiance, energy, and joys of nature's temporal treasures. Working with just a few fabrics, each backed with fusible web, you'll cut rounds of petals. Sue says, "I really enjoy the process of cutting out each completely circular design," but folding each fabric into quarters, as described here, will certainly accelerate your flowers' rate of growth. Either way, the fun part is arranging the tiers in concentric rounds. Each stunning bloom looks impossibly complex—but isn't!

Sue often scavenges and recycles thrift-shop silk and rayon blouses, but cotton in a variety of prints would also work. For the first time in published form, Sue shares her unique methods for growing a profusion of posies, composing a one-of-a-kind art quilt, and binding the edges with satin-stitched simplicity.

Finished measurements: 12" x 60"

materials

Fabrics for the quilt top may be any thin, lightweight fabric, such as silk, rayon, or polyester, as well as 100% cotton (see "Fabric Collecting for Flower Arranging" on page 84). Prewash fabrics, especially recycled clothing.

13" x 26" piece OR two 13" squares *each* of at least 5 different fabrics for quilt top. (Sue used 9 different fabrics to obtain lots of options. She created a total of 7 blocks with leftover pieces and combined the 5 blocks that looked best together, reserving 2 for a separate project.)

17"-wide lightweight paper-backed fusible web. You will need 2 yards for the backing plus ¾ yard for *each* fabric used for the quilt top.

16" x 64" piece of fabric for backing

15" x 63" piece of 100%-cotton batting

Assorted rayon threads for quilting

Template plastic, at least 7" x 14" (gridded is helpful)

Fine-point permanent marker in black and two colors

Craft knife (such as X-acto)

Fabric Collecting for Flower Arranging

- Scout thrift stores and garage sales for silky blouses, skirts, and dresses you can recycle. Torn or stained is no problem with these exciting ingredients for your project.

- Combine shiny and matte, silky and nubby; finely textured fabrics are terrific.

- Pick cotton, silk, linen, rayon, and polyester; sheers like chiffon and organza work, too.

- Choose a range of color values from light to dark. Stretch yourself with unusual selections of brights, tints, tones, and shades.

- Be bold with color, but don't forget to incorporate some neutrals—even black.

- Vary the scale and type of pattern: large-scale, small-scale, abstract, mottled, floral, and geometric prints (but avoid striped fabrics).

making the blocks

1. Cut two 6¼" squares from template plastic. Place a square on each of the patterns on pages 87 and 88, aligning the edges. Using a black marker for the cutting lines and a different color for the radiating guide lines of each pattern (shown in blue), trace the patterns onto the squares. Using either a craft knife or small, sharp scissors, cut along the black lines to produce a wedge with a 90° angle, plus a series of quarter rings with various petal-shaped edges (hereafter called quarter petal rings). Realign cut pieces on the work surface using the guidelines as references.

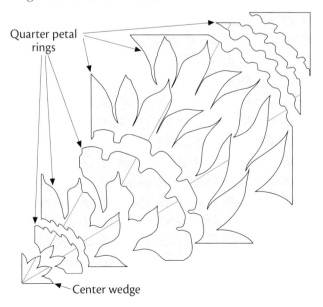

Quarter petal rings

Center wedge

2. Cut two squares, 13" x 13", from fusible web, for *each* fabric for the quilt top. Press two squares of fusible web onto the back of each fabric. Rotary cut two squares, 12½" x 12½", from the fused area of each fabric.

3. Set aside five to seven different squares with paper-backed fusible web on the back for the block backgrounds. It's best to make an extra block or two to provide options for composing the final piece.

4. Fold each of the remaining squares into quarters with the paper side out and the center at the bottom left. Place one of the smallest template quarter-flower wedges on top, matching the center. Trace around the outer edge with a pencil. Next, choose a quarter-petal ring, and position it on the quartered fabric. Check that the left and bottom edges are lined up with the folds, like hands of a clock pointing to 12 and 3 o'clock. Also note that the inside colored guidelines should align with 1 and 2 o'clock. Trace along the inside edge, outside edge, or both edges. Repeat with one, two, or even three more quarter petal rings.

5. Cut out the pieces along the traced lines, taking care to cut through all four layers. Unfold the petal rings and keep them together on the work surface.

6. Trace and cut the other fused squares in the same manner, varying the petal rings. Use pieces from either template, trace different edges each time, or cut freehand, using the traced line merely as a guide for the curve.

7. Lay out all the background squares. Arrange petal rings from non-matching fabrics on top, varying the shapes and colors. Keep building up layers and rearranging pieces until you are satisfied with the resulting flowers. You will have petal rings left over; save them for another project.

8. Remove the paper backing from each petal ring. If, in this process, edges become distorted, trim them as needed. Reposition the petal rings on the background as before, centering carefully.

9. Fuse each block. Take care to reduce the iron temperature for synthetics, or use a Teflon pressing sheet. Fuse again with a pressing cloth and higher heat.

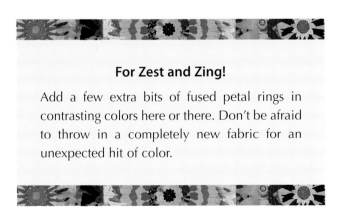

For Zest and Zing!

Add a few extra bits of fused petal rings in contrasting colors here or there. Don't be afraid to throw in a completely new fabric for an unexpected hit of color.

assembling the skinny quilt

1. Arrange the blocks in one row. If you have one or two extra blocks, decide which ones are not as effective, or do not work as well with the others, and eliminate them.

2. Make a "quilt canvas." Cut a piece of fusible web 15" x 63" and fuse it to the wrong side of the backing fabric. Let it cool and then remove the paper backing. Fuse the batting to the fused side of the backing, using steam. Trim the batting and backing to measure 14" x 62".

3. Using a marker, draw a 12" x 60" rectangle centered on the batting side of the quilt canvas. Mark 12" intervals along each 60" side and connect them with crosswise guidelines.

4. Peel the paper backing off of the flower blocks. Fuse the flower blocks at each end so that the blocks overlap the marked lines by ¼".

5. On each of the two blocks next to the end blocks, trim ¼" off the inner edge of the block on the side that touches the end block. Place this trimmed edge so it overlaps the inside edge of the end blocks by ¼". Also, use the guidelines marked on the batting to make sure the placement is straight and true. Fuse these two blocks to the quilt canvas. Trim ¼" from two opposite sides of the center flower block. Position the trimmed edges so they overlap inner edges of the adjacent flower blocks by ¼"; fuse it in place.

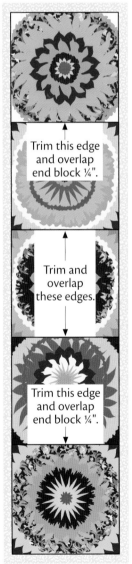

quilting and finishing

Refer to "Quiltmaking Basics and More" on page 89 as needed.

1. Machine quilt as follows, or as desired, using a different color rayon thread for each block. Stitch along overlapping edges between blocks and in lines radiating outward from the center horizontally, vertically, and on both diagonals. Free-motion stitch spirals, beginning at the center of each block and continuing a presser-foot's width apart until the spiral is 6½" in diameter. From there, free-motion stitch around the spiral in long petal shapes. Fill in with curvey lines in the corners.

2. Trim the Skinny Quilt to 12" x 60", and block it to shape again. Refer to "Quiltmaking Basics and More" for blocking instructions if needed. Remember to use a pressing sheet to prevent any synthetics from melting under the heat of the iron.

3. In lieu of binding, satin-stitch the edges. Using one color of thread, leave a long tail of thread, start at one corner, and satin stitch along one side of the quilt. Leave a long tail and cut the thread. Repeat on each edge. Repeat again, making the satin stitches finer and wider. Next, use a contrasting color thread and an open zigzag stitch to go over the stitches on each side twice, for a total of four passes on each edge. Finally, gather all the thread ends at each corner and make a knot; use a pin to slide the knot up tight to the corner. Clip the thread ends, leaving a 2" tassel.

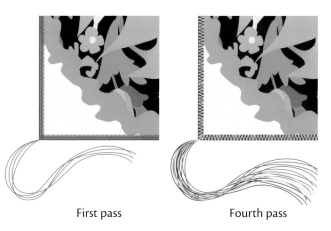

First pass   Fourth pass

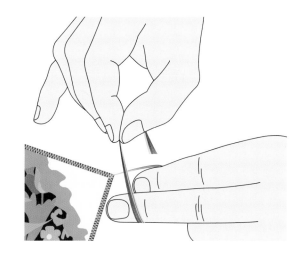

4. Steam press the quilt from the back, flattening out any waves in the edges.

Center

Center

quiltmaking BASICS and more

Get the skinny here on general techniques and extra tips! Beginners: read over this before you begin a project. Experienced quilters: refer to this info on an as-needed basis.

for material girls (and guys)

Yardage amounts for quilter's cottons are based on 42" widths unless otherwise indicated. When possible, the project instructions suggest fat quarters (18" x 21") or fat eighths (9" x 21"). Prewash all cotton fabrics with hot water, and dry in the dryer to preshrink them—loosely woven fabrics, such as flannel, will shrink a lot—and to remove excess dyes. Always remove the selvages—the tightly woven, lengthwise edges of the yardage.

don't want no fat batts here

It's a rare Skinny Quilt that looks puffy. Think about whether you want a nice hand for draping over the edge of a table, or firmness for hanging straight and flat on a wall. Look to your favorite thin battings or splurge on something special—after all, you don't need a lot! Wool and bamboo battings are pricier, but worth it. Also, you may want to forgo batting altogether (see page 26), or consider flannel, interfacing, or felt for the filler. Fusibles will make sandwiching your quilt a cinch.

supplies, supplies!

Here's what you'll want to have handy:

- Paper, tracing paper, and freezer paper, for patterns
- Rotary-cutting supplies (see "Cut to the Chase" at right)
- Sewing machine in good working order
- Thread snips or small embroidery scissors
- Pins, especially flat flower pins, so you can place a rotary ruler on top
- Pincushion

- Fabric markers for light and dark fabrics (Always test them on your fabrics before you use them to be sure the marks will come out.)
- Seam ripper for those inevitable "oops" moments, and tweezers for pulling out threads
- Steam iron, ironing surface, and Teflon, or nonstick pressing sheet (see "Pressing Issues" on page 90)

In addition, the project instructions may list other supplies you'll need for that project.

cut to the chase

Most projects in this book involve rotary cutting and require a cutter with a 45 mm blade, a cutting mat, and acrylic rulers. For your cutting mat, the larger the better, and two or even three 24" x 36" cutting mats placed end to end are great, especially for squaring up your quilt before the binding is added. As to rulers, a 15" square and a 6" x 24" rectangle will be invaluable for cutting backgrounds, borders, and backings, as well as doing the squaring up accurately.

head for the borders

Border measurements are provided as a guide only. Your quilt may end up a little taller or shorter, fatter or skinnier than the dimensions indicate, depending on your seam allowances, cutting, and pressing techniques. Now, no Skinny Quilt needs to be an exact size, so if you can, wait and measure your quilt top before cutting borders to the exact lengths you need.

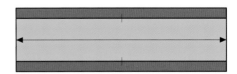

Measure the longest dimension through the center. Mark centers.

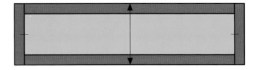

Measure the shortest dimension through the center, including border strips. Mark centers.

piece and harmony

Unless otherwise indicated, place pieces together with right sides facing and edges even. Insert pins at the corners first, at seams that must match, and at intervals in between. Take care to remove pins as your machine needle reaches them; stitching over them will often break the needle. Machine stitch, leaving ¼" seam allowances.

pressing issues

For piecing, you can often finger-press seam allowances until you finish a unit or make multiple units, and then do all the pressing with an iron. Use a hot, dry iron set for cotton, or the setting appropriate for the most temperamental fabric you are using. Never iron directly on metallics, synthetics, or fancy fabrics; use a nonstick pressing cloth as a "go-between."

A Big Fat Ironing Surface

The Big Board is a big help! This 22" x 59" padded surface sits atop your ironing board, where you can lay out your design and do most if not all of your pressing. Or, lean it against a wall, pin elements to it, and stand back to assess your composition. (Available from Big Board Enterprises: bigboardenterprises.com)

fusible appliqué the easy way

Before applying fusible web to fabrics, wash the fabrics to remove any sizing or finishes. Don't use fabric softener, as that will keep you from getting a good bond.

Follow the manufacturer's instructions for the fusible product you are using; in general you will be directed to place fusible web rough side down on the wrong side of your fabric. Protect your iron and ironing surface with a pressing cloth, nonstick pressing sheet, or piece of release paper. Place a hot iron on the fabric for several seconds. Repeat across the surface so that every area of the fabric gets fused.

Cut out fused fabrics with sharp blades—a rotary cutter, or scissors for small, curvy shapes and inset corners. Pin or fuse-tack pieces in place.

When you're ready to secure everything permanently, go to town with the fusing. Set the glue by pressing the quilt top for 10 seconds using a steam iron, or if you prefer, a dry iron and damp pressing cloth. Your iron must be consistently hot—use the cotton setting. Such pressing will provide a good bond between the fabrics and flatten the quilt. Steam press from the back as well.

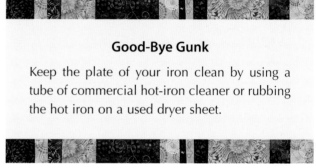

Good-Bye Gunk

Keep the plate of your iron clean by using a tube of commercial hot-iron cleaner or rubbing the hot iron on a used dryer sheet.

machine appliqué and away!

For appliqué or topstitching, use a heavier thread in the needle, such as a 40-weight rayon or cotton. Test your machine's tension, as the fused fabric and background are a firmer surface than usual. Fused appliqués are less prone to ravel, but need at least topstitching to ensure they don't eventually lift. To cover the edges, use decorative stitching. A satin stitch (that is, a narrow zigzag stitch), a blanket stitch, or a buttonhole stitch are great options. If your machine has other decorative stitches, give 'em a whirl!

make a sandwich

Cut batting and backing fabric 2" larger all around than the quilt top. For securing the layers together, basting spray can be a quilter's best friend—but work in a ventilated area, ideally outdoors. Spread out newspapers, an old shower curtain, or something else to catch any overspray. Place the backing right side down on a large, flat surface and spray. Smooth the batting on top. Spray again. Center the quilt top right side up over the batting and backing.

As an alternative to spraying, use giant basting stitches, safety pins, or even straight pins to keep the layers from shifting.

quilt without guilt

Hand quilters: no hoop necessary for Skinny Quilts. Machine quilters: no big bulky piece to squeeze within the harp of the machine and definitely no long-arm needed.

In a rush to finish? Stitch in the ditch with a walking foot, going around the major elements of your Skinny Quilt. Care to add more pattern and color to your quilt? Do it with an open-toe embroidery foot and use any decorative machine stitches your machine can do. Cover raw edges with satin stitching that quilts simultaneously.

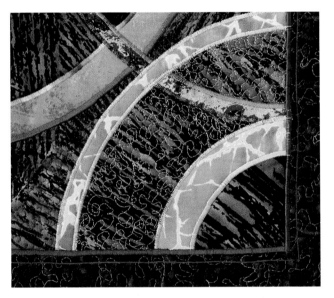

Satin stitching covers raw edges and quilts at the same time on "Seasons of the Moon" (page 32).

For free-motion quilting, some quilters prefer to lower, or at least cover, the feed dogs on their machine. But the key to this popular technique is a darning foot, which allows you to move the quilt sandwich in any direction. The trick, unless you have a sewing machine with a stitch regulator, is getting stitches that are consistent in length. The rate at which you move the piece and run the machine must be smooth, consistent, and compatible. This takes a lot of practice, so experiment on a test piece that is similar in thickness to your project until you are comfortable with the technique.

Free-motion quilting can follow a marked pattern, like the continuous-line design used in the turquoise triangles of "The Dahlia is a Diva" on page 36.

Curlicues and echo curves on "Flowing Lines" (page 48)

Or, it can be truly freehand, meandering over the surface to fill the space nicely, like these examples:

Clamshell design on House block of "An American in Paris" (page 62)

Background texture on "Blushing Aspens" (page 52)

Circling Around

A smooth, curvy circle or arc is a nice complement to a tall, skinny quilt. Here's a small roundup of low-tech tricks for drafting circles of any size:

- **Drafting compass:** Use one with a crossbar and a small wheel between the arms to scribe accurate circles up to 6" in diameter.

- **Yardstick compass:** For larger circles, purchase a kit (available where art and drafting supplies are sold) that includes clips for a pivot point and a lead point. Slip these clips over any yardstick or ruler, adjusting the distance between them for the radius you want.

- **String compass:** Tie a length of string around a pencil. Measure and place a pushpin through the string at the correct length for the pivot point. Swing the pencil around, keeping the string pulled taut.

- **Paper folding:** Cut a square of paper for the diameter of the circle you want. Fold the paper in half, then into quarters, then into a one-eighth wedge, and if possible, a one-sixteenth wedge. Trim across the cut edges in a gentle curve, making the folded edges the same length.

- **Round items:** Trace around a jar lid, dish, plate, platter, bowl, or other round item that gives you the size circle you want.

just a little off the top

After quilting, trim the long edges, and then the short edges of your Skinny Quilt. Use large rulers, fold the quilt in half, and check that your Skinny is absolutely square using the grid on the cutting mat as a guide.

play hangman—or hang woman

If your Skinny Quilt will hang on a wall, you'll want to make a sleeve or casing for a rod. Cut a rectangle of fabric 3" shorter than the top edge of the quilt and 4½" wide. Hem the short ends of the rectangle, fold it lengthwise in half, and lightly press. Center it along the top edge of the backing, with raw edges even. As you bind your quilt, these raw edges will be enclosed. After the binding is attached, slip-stitch along the bottom fold of the casing to secure it to the backing. For a Skinny Quilt that hangs flat, include a narrower rod pocket at the bottom to encase a thin aluminum slat or rod.

bound for glory

Individual project instructions indicate the width and number of strips to cut for a generous amount of binding to go around the quilt.

1. Piece the strips with diagonal seams, and press the seam allowances open.

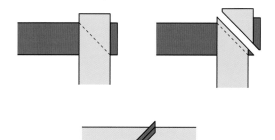

2. Trim the starting end of the binding strip at a 45° angle and fold it under to make a small hem. For a single-fold binding, press one long edge ¼" to the wrong side. For a double-fold binding, press the strip in half lengthwise, wrong sides together.

3. Start at the bottom of the quilt, a few inches from a corner, and leave a 5" tail. With raw edges aligned, pin the long unfolded edge of the single-fold binding or the double raw edges of the double-fold binding to the quilt top. Use a ¼" seam allowance to stitch the binding to the quilt, removing pins as you come to them.

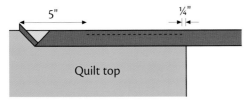

4. To miter the corners, stop stitching ¼" from a corner and take a backstitch. Remove the quilt from under the presser foot and fold the binding up so it's flush with the adjacent edge. Fold the binding down again, alongside the new edge. Insert the needle ¼" from both sides, take a couple of stitches, backstitch, and then continue stitching to the next corner.

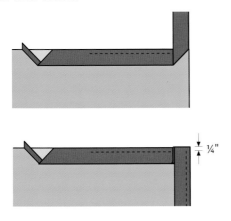

5. When you approach the place where you began, overlap the end of the binding with the folded starting end; trim the finishing end of the binding at a 45° angle. Finish sewing the binding to the quilt.

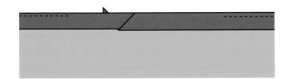

6. Bring the folded edge of the binding over the edges of the quilt sandwich and pin it to the backing. Use thread in a color that matches the binding and slip-stitch along the fold to cover the machine stitching.

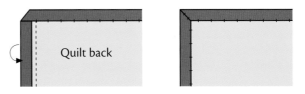

at the finish line

Once the quilt is done, you may need to rinse out any spray starch or any markings you made when cutting, tracing, or quilting.

Finally, only the rare quilt with long edges will come out perfectly even. If you want to get it in shape—and get results that look downright professional—then you've gotta block your quilt. Here's how: Spray the quilt with water and lay it on a large ironing surface that's marked or taped to indicate the proper dimensions all around. Freezer paper, cut to the right size and shiny side up, works perfectly for Skinny Quilts! Gently stretch the edges of your quilt as needed to correspond with your desired dimensions, and pin them to the surface at 2" intervals all around. Steam press or let dry naturally and thoroughly. Leave the pins in for at least 24 hours.

Don't stop until you've signed and dated your work! A lot of contemporary artists use free-motion stitchery to write their signature and the year on the front of the quilt, at the bottom—just as fine-art painters sign their work.

For more traditional documentation, make a label for the back. Include your name, the title of the Skinny Quilt, and the date. If this is a gift, consider adding a brief but personal message for the receiver, such as, "To Mom & Dad on their 50th anniversary." Either fuse the label to the back, or turn the edges under and slip-stitch them in place, penetrating the backing only.

Hooray! Your Skinny Quilt is done!

resources

Check your local quilt shop for fabrics and tools used in this book. For further assistance, use the contacts listed below.

Four-O'Clock Folk Art (page 26)

A complete fabric and embellishment pack for this project, as well as individual felted wool pieces or bundles of felted wool are available from Sue Spargo Folk-Art Quilts, 1364 Walnut Ridge Drive, Uniontown, OH 44685; phone 330-899-9454; www.suespargo. com.

Seasons of the Moon (page 32)

Kits containing Lonni's Paintbox Fabrics in Earthtones & Pastels are available from Lonni Rossi Fabrics, 70 Rittenhouse Place, Ardmore, PA 19003; phone 610-896-0500; www.lonnirossi.com. Lonni also carries the standard Cut A Round tool by Cheryl Phillips for making 6" to 19" circles, or you can contact www.phillipsfiberart.com.

Flowing Lines (page 48)

Silk dupioni is available from Country Keepsakes, RR1, Box 198G, Rome, PA 18837; phone 570-744-2246; www.countrykeepsakesonline.com (click on Online Catalog then Silk Dupioni at the left).

Blushing Aspens (page 52)

Frieda Anderson's hand-dyed fabrics are available by contacting her at 1995 Murcer, Elgin, IL 60123; phone 847-697-6557; www.friestyle.com.

Wisteria Lane (page 70)

For the location of a supplier of Steam-A-Seam 2, contact The Warm Company, 5529 186th Place SW, Lynnwood, WA 98037; phone 425-248-2424; www.warmcompany.com.

Waking Up, Down the Shore (page 76)

Contact Benartex at www.benartex.com for the location of stores carrying Gradations by Caryl Bryer Fallert, or contact Caryl at www.bryerpatch.com for full-yard cuts. See "Flowing Lines" above for a source for silk dupioni.

about the DESIGNERS

Karla Alexander (www.saginawstreet-quilts.com) lives in beautiful Salem, Oregon, with her husband, Don, the youngest of their three sons, William, and the family dog, Lucy. Karla is the author of several books, including *Stack the Deck!* and *Stack a New Deck!* (both published by Martingale & Company). Her company, the Saginaw Street Quilt Company—named for the address where she lived when she started her business—also has a line of patterns. She has taught thousands of students how to quilt using her popular stack methods, plus a variety of other easy and innovative shortcuts.

Frieda Anderson (www.friestyle.com) discovered hand dyeing and now works almost exclusively with her own hand-dyed cottons and silks. She revels in the colors emerging from the wet fabric. As a faculty member of the fictitious Chicago School of Fusing, Frieda is pleased to use fusing as part of her repertoire that also lists piecing and free-motion quilting as points of pride.

Sue Benner (www.suebenner.com) is an innovative quilt artist, creating original dyed and painted fabrics that she combines with recycled textiles for art that is in many private, corporate, and institutional collections. She lectures and teaches workshops in surface design, textile collage, fused quilt construction, and artistic inspiration. While born and raised in Wisconsin, Sue lives in Dallas, Texas, with her husband and their two sons.

Melinda Bula (www.melindabula. com) is a former flight attendant who has also flown high as a fabric and wallpaper designer. Her silk-screened home-decor creations have graced the covers of *Better Homes and Gardens* and *Sunset* magazines. Melinda indulges in glorious color in her book, *Cutting-Garden Quilts* (Martingale & Company) and at Melinda Bula Designs, a line of patterns that includes redwork, appliqué, and wearables.

Jane Dávila (www.janedavila.com) is a fiber and mixed-media artist who began her professional career as a printmaker. Her work can be found in many private and corporate collections worldwide. Jane is an author, and she teaches art quilting and surface design workshops nationally. She lives in Ridgefield, Connecticut, with her husband, Carlos, an abstract artist whose medium is oil paint.

Joanna Figueroa (www.figtreequilts. com) is the talent behind Fig Tree & Co. She designs fabric collections for Moda, as well as dozens of quilting patterns, and is the author of *Fig Tree Quilts: Fresh Vintage Sewing* and *Fig Tree Quilts: Houses* (with Lisa Quan). She travels regularly for national and European teaching engagements and organizes regular trunk shows of her work. In addition, her company publishes Fresh Vintage, a pattern publication that also gives customers an insight into her design process.

Judy Hooworth lives just north of Sydney, Australia. Her modern takes on pieced traditions have been showcased in three books, most recently *Quilts on the Double* (Martingale & Company). Her masterworks have been featured four times in Quilt National. Judy teaches patchwork and quilting and helps students develop a personal vocabulary for art quilts.

Linda Lum DeBono (www.lindalum-debono.com) infuses her quilting with fashion sense, modern color, and whimsy. She designs fabric for Henry Glass & Company, as well as sewn and quilted projects for books and magazines. Two school-aged children have inspired designs for babies and tots, plus ideas for younger fans taking up the needle, such as *Cool Girls Quilt* (Martingale & Company) and trendy looks for home decor. Oh, and she designs knitted accessories. About the only thing Linda doesn't like to do is housework!

Jo Morton (www.jomortonquilts.com) studies antique quilts for quirks and for color or design to use as a source of inspiration for her own interpretations. Each of her works is destined to be a long-lasting heirloom; however, they're invariably made using new cotton fabrics, most often the reproduction fabrics designed by Jo for Andover Fabrics. She teaches and lectures for quilt guilds, shops, and retreats. Via Jo's Little Women Clubs, she invites fans of yesteryear's charms to step back in time, join an old-fashioned gathering at a local quilt shop, and make "small, olde-looking quilts and needful things."

Julie Popa (www.sunflowerhilldesigns. com) has used the design principles she learned as a student of interior design to turn her quilting hobby into a profession. Julie founded Sunflower Hill Designs in 2001 to market her diverse group of patterns and books, which include *A Fresh Look at Seasonal Quilts* (Martingale & Company). Julie, her husband, and their four children make their home in Smithfield, Utah.

Elizabeth Rosenberg (www.eliza-bethrosenberg.com) used to be a backup singer for, as she puts it, "rock and roll artists you've never heard of." Nowadays, her creative and highly improvisational talents are focused on what she calls "paintings made of fabric." Her award-winning art quilts regularly feature free-flowing lines and free-motion quilting. She teaches workshops such as "Free Motion without Fear" and presents lectures such as "My Love Affair with the Flowing Line."

Lonni Rossi (www.lonnirossi.com) is a former graphic designer, and her fascination with fonts, typography, text, photography, and graphics makes them frequent players in many of her fabrics—hand-painted, stamped, and silk-screened, as well as the fabric collections she designs for Andover Fabrics. The Lonni Rossi Fabrics studio and shop, which carries her unique and commercial fabrics, plus others with a similar contemporary flair, is in Main Line, Philadelphia, close to the home she shares with her husband.

Karen Costello Soltys has been quilting since 1979 when she took her first class. Since then, Karen has made countless quilts for family, friends, and charitable causes, mostly using machine techniques, but also including hand appliqué and hand quilting. Over the past 15 years, she has edited many quilting books and has contributed quilts to other authors' books. She is the author of *Bits and Pieces* (Martingale & Company). Karen's love for traditional needlework extends to primitive rug hooking, knitting, and basket making.

Sue Spargo (www.suespargo.com) was born in Zambia, schooled in South Africa, and worked as a nurse in England. She has lived in Connecticut, Tennessee, Utah, and now resides in a small town in northeastern Ohio. She credits all the places she's lived for helping her to develop her unique style of folk art. Sue has designed patterns and written books and teaches workshops at quilting shows and retreats. With her sister, Wendy Morris, Sue creates the Earthworks range of hand-dyed wool, velvet, silk, and linen fabrics. They also collaborate to translate Sue's folk-art designs into silver jewelry.

about the EDITOR

Eleanor Levie (www.eleanorlevie.com) has run with the best during three decades as a needlework and crafts editor, author, book producer, and photo stylist, with quilting as her specialty. After enjoying countless chances to learn from the experts while editing their books and chapters, Elly loves to synthesize and combine all manner of techniques in her own eclectic quilting. When she's not running up how-to instructions on her home computer or running her sewing machine, she's often running on about quilting in presentations for quilt guilds and groups. While she rhapsodizes about the joys of making and decorating with quilts, she puts special focus on quilts in which the maker pushed the envelope, stretched the limits, and dared to be different. In trunk shows and slides of the historical, hysterical, and contemporary, Elly preaches that quilts can be both art *and* craft. And in workshops that are more like playdates, she teaches crafty techniques that are enormous fun for both new and experienced quilters.

This lover of Skinny Quilts and table runners is herself a runner—running on a treadmill, running over the tennis court, or running to keep up with her hubby. Gorgeous days inspire hikes around their home base of Bucks County, Pennsylvania, and serve as training for trips to farther-flung places.

Portrait by Great Circle Photography of Doylestown, Pennsylvania